Yale Studies in English, 173

Milton and the Idea of Matrimony

A Study of the
Divorce Tracts and *Paradise Lost*

by John Halkett

New Haven and London, Yale University Press, 1970

Published with assistance from
the foundation established in memory
of Philip Hamilton McMillan of the
Class of 1894, Yale College.
Copyright © 1970 by Yale University.
All rights reserved. This book may not be
reproduced, in whole or in part, in any form
(except by reviewers for the public press),
without written permission from the publishers.
Library of Congress catalog card number: 71–99825
Standard book number: 300–0–1196–2
Designed by Marvin Howard Simmons,
set in Baskerville type,
and printed in the United States of America by
The Carl Purington Rollins Printing-Office of the
Yale University Press, New Haven, Connecticut.
Distributed in Great Britain, Europe, Asia, and
Africa by Yale University Press Ltd., London; in
Canada by McGill-Queen's University Press, Montreal; and
in Mexico by Centro Interamericano de Libros
Académicos, Mexico City.

Contents

Preface

This is not the first work to be addressed to the concept of matrimony in Milton, nor, considering its limitations, could one wish it to be the last. It is mainly concerned with a special question—the extent to which the ideal of matrimony in Milton's divorce tracts is embodied in *Paradise Lost*. But it also attempts to reveal in what way Milton's tracts accept, deny, modify, or exploit popular, and especially "Puritan," notions of the marriage relationship. Close attention is paid to the wavering correspondences between word and concept in the practical literature of marriage, the best surviving indication of popular attitudes. Such a study of Milton's tracts against the popular background has implications for the reading of *Paradise Lost,* since one has learned before approaching the poem both Milton's explicit theorctical positions in the ethical controversy which lay behind the passages dealing with marriage and something of the spirit in which those passages must have been received by Milton's audience.

Scholarly work has, of course, been done on the background of the divorce tracts. That of William and Malleville Haller and of Roland Mushat Frye is discussed in the text, and my indebtedness to their studies as well as to Louis B. Wright's *Middle Class Culture in Elizabethan England* (Chapel Hill, 1935) is very great indeed. I have not found it necessary to rehearse most of their generalizations, and those which have provided me with points of debate I have been grateful for. The Hallers' sense of the emotional correspondence between Milton's attitude toward matrimony and the attitudes of most contemporary Puritan preachers has real validity; the impression which might be gathered from their essays and which I would like to correct is that Milton's arguments rested on solid verbal or conceptual grounds in the preachers. I feel that they did not, and that the suspicion with which Milton's radical ideas were regarded by his contemporaries was perfectly consistent with his idiosyncratic use of the biblical texts as well as the concepts and vocabulary of matrimonial literature.

Other works have proved useful in investigating certain phases of the topic, but examples of overlapping interests are few. Chilton Latham Powell's *English Domestic Relations, 1487–1653* (New York, 1917), a broad survey of matrimony "as revealed by the literature, law, and history of the period," is concerned with the legal form of the marriage ceremony and with the Renaissance conception of the contract rather than the nature of marriage. The focus of his work falls upon the debate as to which institution, civil or ecclesiastical, had the right of jurisdiction over the contract. Ernest Sirluck's introduction to the divorce pamphlets in the Yale edition of Milton's prose (vol. 2, New Haven, 1959) closely analyzes the significant immediate influences on Milton's argument. But Sirluck deals with the Parliamentary debates and their fluctuating common assumptions rather than with the influence of Puritan attitudes toward marriage. Arthur Barker's *Milton and the Puritan Dilemma, 1641–1660* (Toronto, 1942), useful for an understanding of Milton's concept of law, approaches the divorce tracts as a stage in Milton's development of the concept of Christian liberty. "John Milton's Pamphlets on Divorce," a doctoral dissertation by Lester Deane Moody (University of Washington, 1956), is essentially a gloss of all the proper names in the text, but it also contains a rhetorical analysis of *The Doctrine and Discipline of Divorce* (1644); the method is that of W. E. Gilman's *Milton's Rhetoric* (Columbia, Mo., 1939), that is, an outline and a classification of arguments according to the Aristotelian categories of proof—logical, ethical, and pathetic.

There are two analyses of the language and imagery of the

tracts. Kester Svendsen's "Science and Structure in Milton's
Doctrine of Divorce" (*PMLA*, 67 [1952], 435–45) examines the
anatomical and astronomical imagery of *The Doctrine and
Discipline of Divorce* (1644). For Svendsen, Milton's association
of his own ideas with health or order and his opponents' ideas
with disease or chaos is, in effect, the argument. There is the
same reluctance to treat assertions as ideas in Thomas Kranidas'
The Fierce Equation: A Study of Milton's Decorum (The
Hague, 1965). Both studies, however, throw light on the range
and unifying force of Milton's rhetoric.

Finally, Arthur M. Axelrad's dissertation "One Gentle Stroking: Milton on Divorce" (New York University, 1962) takes
up, at least tangentially, the vexed and in many ways insoluble
problem of the relationship between Milton's first marriage
and his theoretical stance in the divorce tracts. Axelrad's first
chapter is derived from Powell, but his second chapter considers
Milton's reading in the divorce question and the possible reasons for his failure to make reference to this reading in the
tracts: it was either not influential or not germane to his argument. Axelrad gives thorough attention to the logical method
of the tracts and to Milton's acquaintance with Anglo-Saxon
divorce law.

My own concern with the vocabulary and definitions of the
theoretical and practical literature of marriage will, I hope,
further the knowledge and the speculation to which these works
have contributed. My comments on the relationship between the
divorce tracts and *Paradise Lost* do not pretend to exhaust the
questions posed by the works themselves.

The texts of the quotations which I have used follow the
editions cited. Short titles are generally used in the text and the
footnotes; longer titles are supplied in the bibliography. I am
grateful to the staffs of the libraries at Northwestern and Yale,
the Newberry Library, and the British Museum. And for their
patience and encouragement I would like to thank my dissertation adviser, Zera S. Fink of Northwestern, and Louis L. Martz,
George de F. Lord, and Richard S. Sylvester of Yale, who read
the manuscript.

I

Matrimonium Quid:

Definitions of Marriage.

The Ends of Marriage.

"We need a definition."
"Well then, follow me if you think I will make a decent guide."
"Lead the way."

Plato, *The Republic,* V, 474

Milton's four tractates on divorce—*The Doctrine and Discipline of Divorce* (1643, revised and expanded 1644), *The Judgment of Martin Bucer* (1644), *Tetrachordon* (1645), and *Colasterion* (1645)—occupy a crucial place in the canon. Their theoretical postulates indicate that Milton had severed his connection with the Presbyterians, whom he had defended in the Smectymnuan controversy of 1641. In the divorce tracts, Milton argues for a reform of marriage law in a way which outdistances the universally conservative thinking of his contemporaries, whether Anglican or Puritan.[1] But the tracts are crucial in another way as well: they have provided his biographers with a

1. A workable definition of the term "Puritanism" is M. M. Knappen's reduction of Trevelyan's discussion in *England under the Stuarts* (16th ed. London, 1933, pp. 60–71): "Puritanism is 'the religion of all those who wished either to "purify" the usage of the established church from taint of popery or to worship separately by forms so "purified." ' Neither creed nor theory of church government was a distinguishing feature. There were Episcopalian, Presbyterian, and Congregational Puritans. Bibliolatry, a tendency to individualistic interpretation of their authorities, a wariness of gaiety, and a passionate love of civic freedom and moral earnestness are other common-denominator principles." Marshall Mason Knappen, *Tudor Puritanism: A Chapter in the History of Idealism* (Chicago, 1939), p. 489.

rather uncomfortable set of possibilities. Masson's supposition that Milton wrote his first statement of the case for divorce shortly after his honeymoon has been, if not disproved, at least vehemently questioned.[2] But the earliest biographers mention the disparity of temperament between John Milton and Mary Powell, and they assume that Milton was thinking of his own case when he rested his argument for divorce on the assertion that incompatibility as well as adultery or desertion could nullify the marriage bond. The question that puzzles modern biographers, now that we assume a longer period between the marriage and the publication of the first tract, is the extent to which the tracts reflect Milton's personal situation. Hanford claims, with probable justice, that Milton's incidental descriptions of cases of mismating resemble his own.[3]

Do the divorce tracts in fact represent a case of biased pleading? On the one hand, it is possible to see in the tracts as Milton said he conceived them the merely logical outcome of an interest in reforming the laws and ceremonies of his country. In this case, the first divorce tract and Milton's first year of marriage coincide accidentally. On the other hand, it is possible to see nothing but a personal interest in the outcome of the debate which the tracts were to provoke. The usual reconciliation of these contraries is that Milton turned at a moment of grave personal difficulty to a question he had been weighing for a long time; and his passionate and unabated involvement in the argument, which captured his attention for nearly two years, reflects a profound personal concern.

It is probable, however, that Milton's objectivity of purpose exceeds the concessions of his biographers. The tenacity of Milton's effort, the number of his tracts on divorce, and the frequent shift in the details of his argument all indicate a commitment to his cause; but Milton was deeply concerned in every cause he supported, and there is little reason to treat the divorce

2. See James Holly Hanford, *John Milton, Englishman* (New York, 1949), p. 114.
3. Ibid., p. 116.

tracts as a special case of personal implication. If he had really been more interested in divorcing Mary Powell than in arguing the cause of divorce generally, it is unlikely that he would have rested his argument—and rested it long after he might have modified it to his advantage—on the idiosyncratic grounds he chose. For the fact is that no Reformed church allowed divorce on the basis of incompatibility. Yet the Continental reformers did recognize biblical sanctions for divorce in the case of adultery or desertion. The English church alone, which still followed canon law in matrimonial issues, did not yet recognize divorce *a vinculo* at all, for whatever cause. It merely allowed separation in cases of adultery, *a mensa et thoro*.[4] Hence, if England was to be reformed on the Continental model, divorce might be argued with greater effect for causes recognized by the majority of Protestants than for the cause of incompatibility.[5] And Milton, whose wife—according to all accounts except his mother-in-law's—had deserted him, could, if he had argued divorce for desertion, probably have won the debate, influenced the law, and obtained his freedom. If Milton had been chiefly concerned with his own situation, it would seem perverse of him to adopt an extreme position which had little chance of winning the day. We must assume that whatever personal involvement there is in the tracts lies in Milton's convictions about the nature of marriage, convictions perhaps more forcefully present to him because of his own thwarted and unhappy experience. His experience may have helped to shape those convictions, but it is inaccurate to read the tracts as largely personal documents; the pressure of conviction operates at a higher level of abstraction, and the special case, including Milton's own, becomes relatively unimportant as a part of the argument.

If biographers have shown a continuing and necessary in-

4. The reformers Fagius and Bucer had, in the time of Edward VI, advocated a change in the laws which was never acted upon. See William and Malleville Haller, "The Puritan Art of Love," *Huntington Library Quarterly*, 5 (1942), 239.

5. This point is made by Arthur Axelrad, "One Gentle Stroking," p. 17.

terest in Milton's divorce tracts, investigations of the argument
they contain have been less frequent. The most reliable and
useful of these are the essays by William Haller which trace the
classical, biblical, and Puritan background of the tracts.[6] Haller's contention is that the Puritan preachers, by stressing the
role of the married woman in their sermons, treatises, and conduct books, helped to form in the minds of their audience a
relatively modern concept of marriage as a partnership of love
and mutual helpfulness. Milton's concept of marriage, therefore, owes as much to his religious training as to Plato or
Spenser, and it expresses a widespread attitude toward marriage,
merely carrying the principles of Puritan domestic theory to
their logical fulfillment:

> though Milton voiced the accepted tenets of Puritan doc-
> trine, he did not draw back as the preachers did from its
> extreme implications. We have seen that, as the preachers
> went on elaborating the doctrine of marriage, they tended
> more and more to speak as though the indispensable end of
> matrimony were less to relieve the body and beget children
> than to console the spirit, as though the essential constituents
> of the marital union were not so much authority and sub-
> jection as sympathy and love.[7]

This is a cautious, judicious, and moderate statement of a principle first enunciated by Chilton Latham Powell; Powell con-
tended that Milton's redefinition of the grounds of divorce "was
but a logical result of the Puritan attitude towards marriage
according to which matrimony was instituted for the mutual
blessing and benefit of husband and wife instead of for the
procreation of children and the avoidance of sin."[8]

6. William and Malleville Haller, "Puritan Art of Love," p. 239; William
Haller: *The Rise of Puritanism* (New York, 1938); "Hail Wedded Love,"
English Literary History, 13 (1946), 79–97; *Liberty and Reformation in the
Puritan Revolution* (New York, 1955).

7. William and Malleville Haller, "Puritan Art of Love," p. 270. See also
Haller, "Hail Wedded Love," p. 82.

8. *English Domestic Relations,* p. 94.

Both Haller and Powell attempt to account for Milton's idea
of marriage in terms of a milieu which they define as "Puritan."
But there are certain difficulties attending this view of the
matter which bear investigation. One is that no Puritan writer
ever states flatly that mutual help is the primary end of marriage
as such, although woman was man's "meet help." Another is
that although there is some consistency in general statements
about marriage on the part of Puritan writers ("marriage is
honorable in all") there is no discernible agreement in en-
thusiasm. Marriage could be the pathway to salvation or "a little
hel." Preachers could try to convert the latter sort of marriage
into the former, but not all of them celebrate marriage as the
most prudent condition of man in the fallen world. Some, like
Richard Baxter, look upon virginity as the more desirable
state, for ministers at least,[9] and others, like William Whately
and Alexander Niccholes, seem less than complacent about the
crosses of marriage. A third difficulty is that there is no clear
distinction between Puritan and Anglican teaching on marriage.[10] A fourth is that a theory of conjugal love based on
"affinity," which the writers of courtesy books usually set forward (if we must see Milton's attitudes in terms of a popular
genre), seems closer to Milton's position than do the definitions
of Puritan writers. And a final peculiarity is that Milton's concept of what could and could not be changed in human beings
by effort of will seems, in the divorce tracts at least, not to correspond to the common Puritan doctrine of marriage.

9. *The Christian Directory* (London, 1673), pp. 475–76.
10. Lady Dorothy Packington's *The Whole Duty of Man* (London, 1660),
in its insistence on love and sympathy, sounds as "Puritan" as any of the
works which Haller cites: "[the wife] owes [her husband] *love,* and together
with that all friendliness and kindness of conversation; she is to endeavour
to bring him as much assistance, and comfort of life, as is possible, that so
she may answer that special end of the woman's creation, the being *a help
to her husband*" (p. 313). The preface to this work, dated 1657, was written
by the Anglican and Royalist preacher Henry Hammond, and the actual
author of the work itself, according to the *Dictionary of National Biography,*
may have been Richard Allestree, a divine, a Royalist soldier, and a courier
for Charles II.

Evaluations of the attitudes of Milton and the Puritans toward marriage or divorce inevitably merge with encomia based
on the predilections of the critic. "Modernity,"[11] idealism,[12]
and the recognition of conjugal sexuality[13] furnish standards
by which praise can be directed and liberally dispensed. It
would be difficult not to honor the past for taking a position
which can be made to harmonize so easily with the present;
but it is equally true that hindsight creates "advanced" ideas
as such and that Milton's "attitudes" are often essentially persuasive elements in a rhetorical framework. It is sheer historical
accident that the ideal of marriage which he professes is an irre-
proachable goal of the contemporary Anglo-Saxon pursuit of
"happiness." Furthermore, against his demand for compatibility as the norm of marriage we can, if we wish, set his opinion
of natural feminine inferiority, his obvious subordination of
the woman's role in marriage, and the inequities to which
these give rise in his pronouncements on divorce—attitudes
which do not consort so comfortably with modern prejudice.
Nonetheless, Milton's tractates on divorce are not more remarkable for their argumentative method and their assumptions
about human nature than for special attitudes toward marriage.
In them Milton raises human reason to the level of sole arbiter
of moral issues and the individual to a position of eminence over
institutions, as though particular men could both see and want
their own good. For these reasons, as well as for the intrinsic
interest of the problem itself, Milton's attitudes toward marriage need to be evaluated in terms of their particular historical
context.

The Puritan temper has in the last half-century undergone
a form of scholarly redemption. Thanks to C. L. Powell, M. M.
Knappen, William and Malleville Haller, Edmund S. Morgan,

11. Martin Alfred Larson, *The Modernity of Milton* (Chicago, 1927),
pp. 244–59.

12. Ian Watt, *The Rise of the Modern Novel* (Berkeley, 1957), p. 137.

13. Roland Mushat Frye, "The Teachings of Classical Puritanism on Conjugal Love," *Studies in the Renaissance, 2* (1955), 148–59.

Charles and Katherine George, and others, it is no longer fashionable to think of the Puritan as a repressed and restrictive fundamentalist. His "image" is now that of the enlightened progressive, fearing, it may be, the possibility of reprobation, but performing an existentialist drama in which the right gestures give the actor some assurance of having the right script. This picture of his social bearing and moral dilemmas is attractive to us; we find, to our relief, that the Puritan can be tolerated because he is not much different from ourselves. But the new corporate image is not more universally true than the old. What writers about Puritan attitudes tend to blur in the minds of their readers is that the movement to reform the English church included a wide spectrum of opinions and attitudes, just as it embraced a membership recruited from all social strata. The attempt to give "the Puritan attitude" certain contours—a necessary attempt for the historian—has sometimes resulted in falsifications of the breadth and variety of Puritan opinions. This is nowhere so true as in certain aspects of "the Puritan attitude towards marriage." There is, certainly, a tradition of sentiments and concerns in the Puritan writers; but then they had recourse to the same authorities as Anglican authors, and each writer varied the emphasis, order, and interpretation of the traditional ideas. Both formal definitions of marriage and statements of the ends for which marriage—or woman—was created provide some focus for the examination of these variations. Furthermore, they necessitate certain judgments about the uniqueness of Milton's position.

The formal definition of marriage occupies Milton at some length in *Tetrachordon*.[14] Before he attempts his own definition, he assembles and, in some cases, rejects the opinions of previous authorities, ancient and modern—the Calvinist Paraeus, the English Puritan Ames, the Danish theologian Hemmingus (Hemingius, or Niels Hemmingsen), and the compilers of the

14. John Milton, *Tetrachordon*, ed. Arnold Williams, *Complete Prose Works*, 2, ed. *Don M. Wolfe* (New Haven, 1953), 608–14. The series is hereafter cited as *CPW*.

fifth-century *Institutes* and the third-century *Pandects*—Tribonianus and Modestinus.[15] Paraeus makes all marriages indissoluble per se; Milton objects that every marriage is not a
"true marriage." According to Milton, Ames places physical before spiritual needs; Hemmingus makes one purpose of marriage (unity, whether physical or spiritual) part of its essence
rather than its effect; and Tribonianus and Modestinus make
similar errors, including effects rather than causes as part of
the definition. Milton declares his own definition to be derived
from the text Gen. 2. 24: *"Marlage is a divine institution joyning man and woman in a love fitly dispos'd to the helps and
comforts of domestic life"* (p. 612). The distinctive feature of
Milton's argument is that love and its effects ("the helps and
comforts of domestic life") constitute "the formal cause it self
of mariage." God is the efficient cause, but "love born of fitness," the love which creates domestic peace, is the formal cause.
Milton is absolutely right in asserting the absence of this key
term from all former definitions of marriage (see p. 613),[16] for
in asserting the primacy of human feeling over contractual
rigor he has taken marriage out of the realm of law and placed
it in the realm of affective psychology. The Puritan preachers
may have been concerned with marital affections as necessary
to a happy marriage, but they were by no means willing to assert
that these affections were essential to marriage itself. Milton's
argument declares invalid all marriages in which such a feeling
—or its possibility—is absent.

The definitions which Milton cites are not the only evidence
of contemporary attitudes on the subject. Milton's authorities

15. These authors are glossed in *CPW*, 2, 246, 610, 611, and 611–12, re-
spectively.
16. Cf. Daniel Rogers' distinction between betrothals and marriages: "The
union of contracted ones, is an union of imagination, or of affection, so long
as its within such boundes: But the union of marriage, is an union of state
and condition, standing in right, and law, above all private affection. If
private contracts be broken off . . . there is private satisfaction given to the
parties: but if marriage be broken off, there is publique scandall given beyond all satisfaction." *Matrimoniall Honovr* (London, 1642), p. 116.

had probably been collected for him as commonplace citations.[17] However, there are other sources of equal currency and popularity. Some of them, like Johannes Andrea's *De Sponsalibus et Matrimoniis*,[18] are digests of learned opinion. Andrea's definitions of marriage are obviously derived from the *Institutes* and the *Pandects* of the *Juris Civilis:* they are equivalent to Milton's versions of Tribonianus and Modestinus and would be offered similar rejoinders:

> Matrimonium est viri et mulieris coniunctio individuam vitae consuetudinem retinens. . . . Aliter diffinitur sic: Matrimonium est viri et feminae consortium: communis vitae divini et humanis iuris coniunctio.[19]

Erasmus, Bullinger, Dod and Cleaver, Henry Smith, and William Perkins, among others familiar to Milton's contemporaries, attempt a definition of marriage. The differences among them bespeak a widely varied set of assumptions, even in the case of Dod and Cleaver, who merely quote Bullinger but then gloss his definition. However, all of them agree about the special nature of the marital contract. The following are the relevant definitions:

> Est enim proprie matrimonium legitima perpetua viri ac mulieris, studio gignendae sobolis, inita coniunctio, vitae ac fortunarum omnium individuā societatē adducēs. [For matrimony is properly a lawful and constant union of bodies of man and wife undertaken in an endeavor to produce offspring, leading to an indivisible fellowship of life and all circumstances.]
>
> Erasmus[20]

17. Arnold Williams, "Preface to Tetrachordon," *CPW*, 2, 573–74.

18. *Summa Johannis Andreae de Sponsalibus et Matrimoniis* (Rome, 1490).

19. Milton's translation of the definitions in the *Institutes* and the *Pandects* are in fact literal translations of these lines as well. See *CPW*, 2, 611.

20. Desiderius Erasmus, *Christiani Matrimonii Institutio* (Basel, 1526), sig. 8ʳ. (My translation; I have emended *adduces to adducēs*.)

Si causam efficiētem scire cupis, audis, legitima coniunctio.
Lex enim autor est veri matrimonij, sed huius legis autor est
deus, qui primus iunxit marem ac foeminā, modo coniugij
leges praescripsit, dicens: Et erū duo in carnem unam. Et,
propter hoc relinquet homo patrem ac matrē, & adhaerebit
uxori suae. Itē, crescite & multiplicamini & replete terram. . . .
Formalem causam accipe, dum audis coniunctionem & so-
cietatem uitae. Nō enim est matrimonium, nisi cōnubialis
animorum consensus intcrucncrit. Uude excludūtur ab hac
formula, stupri societas, & coacta matrimonia. Finis aūt est
propagatio sobolis, unde nec inter effoetos senio, nec inter eos
qui deploratae sunt sterilitatis, verum coit matrimonium,
iuxta propriam & exactam quā nos proposuimus, matrimonij
ratiōnē, tametsi quasdam matrimoniorū species secundae ter-
tiae classis non reijcit Ecclesia. [If you wish to know the efficient cause, you hear it, a lawful union. For law is the creator
of true matrimony, but the creator of this law is God, who first
joined husband and wife and then prescribed the laws of marriage, saying: And they shall be two in one flesh. And for this
shall a man leave his father and mother, and cleave to his
wife. Likewise, increase and multiply, and fill the earth. . . .
Take it as the formal cause when you hear the union and
fellowship of life. For it is not a marriage unless conjugal
agreement of minds has taken place. Wherefore by this principle the society of whoredom and forced marriages are ex-
cluded. The end, however, is the begetting of offspring, for
which reason trüe marriage does not unite those enfeebled
by age or those incurably sterile according to the proper or
exact aim of marriage which we have proposed, although the
church does not reject certain kinds of marriage of the second
or third class.]

Erasmus[21]

Wedlock is a lawfull knot and unto God an acceptable yoking
together of one man and one woman with the good consent

21. Erasmus, sig. b^r–b^v (my translation).

of them both, to the intēt thᾰt they two may dwel together in
friendship and honesty, one helping and comforting the
other, eschuing uncleanes, and bringing up children in y^e
feare of God.

Bullinger[22]

Wedlocke or Matrimony is a lawfull knot, and vnto God
an acceptable yoking and ioyning together of one man and
one woman, with the good consent of them both: to the end
that they may dwell together in friendship and honesty, one
helping and comforting the other, eschuing whoredome, and
all uncleannesse, bringing up their children in the feare of
God: or it is a coupling together of two persons into one
flesh, according to the ordinance of God; not to be broken,
but so to continue during the life of either of them, Gen. 22.
Malach. 2.14. Rom. 7.31.

By yoking, ioyning, or coupling is meant, not only outward
dwelling together of the married folkes, as to bee ordinarily
in a dwelling place for the better performance of mutuall
duties to each other . . . but also an uniforme agreement of
mind and a common participation of body and goods.

Dod and Cleaver[23]

mariage . . . is nothing else but a communion of life between
man and woman ioyned together according to the ordinance
of God.

Smith[24]

Mariage is the lawfull coniunction of the two maried persons; that is, of one man, and one woman into one flesh.

Perkins[25]

22. Henry Bullinger, *The Christian State of Matrimony*, trans. Myles
Coverdale (6th ed. London, 1575), Fol. 5^v–6^v.
23. John Dod and Robert Cleaver, *A Godlie Forme of Household Government* (London, 1612), sig. F8^r–F8^v.
24. Henry Smith, "Preparative to Marriage" in *Sermons* (London, 1622),
p. 9.
25. William Perkins, *Christian Oeconomie* (London, 1609), p. 10.

Bullinger's definition, which contains the three ends for which most writers saw marriage as created, would seem to give some primacy to mutual aid and comfort, except that later in the text, in an analysis of the ends of marriage, he gives actual primacy to procreation.[26] The definitions of Dod and Cleaver, derived from Bullinger, are given a rather significant gloss: "Matrimony then, being an indissoluble bond and knot, whereby the husband and wife are fastened together by the ordinance of God, is farre straighter than any other coiunction in the society of mankind. Insomuch that it is a lesse offence for a man to forsake father and mother, and to leave them succourlesse, (who notwithstanding ought, by Gods commandement to be honoured) then it is for him to doe the like towards his lawful married wife."[27] Marriage thus becomes a more confining and indissoluble bond than bonds of natural kinship. The implications of this position are not, however, adhered to in the position adopted by Dod and Cleaver on divorce. The inconsistency can be explained as a concession to the biblical sanction of divorce for adultery (Matt. 5:32) and to the contemporary Reformation sanction of divorce for desertion.[28]

Perkins and Henry Smith, as well as Dod and Cleaver, speak of "conjunction" and "communion of life," but they omit mention of the causes of the bond; their "defect" is similar to those of Milton's authorities. The phrase "according to the ordinance of God" suggests, as does Dod and Cleaver's definition, a kind of contract which has a special supernatural binding force and is not to be judged according to the usual principles of human contracts.[29] In all cases, even Perkins', the implication of an indissoluble kind of unity is foremost.

26. Bullinger, sig. 25ʳ.
27. Dod and Cleaver, *Household Government*, sig. Gʳ.
28. Ernest Sirluck, "Preface" to *The Doctrine and Discipline of Divorce, CPW*, 2, 157; see also Sir Lewis Didbin and Sir Charles E. H. C. Healey, *English Church Law and Divorce* (London, 1912), p. 44.
29. See William Perkins, *A Commentarie or Exposition upon the First Five Chapters of the Epistle to the Galatians* (1631), *Works* (London, 1626–31), 2, 297.

Erasmus approximates Milton's exposition of efficient, formal, and final causes,[30] but aside from assigning the efficient cause to God the positions differ markedly. For Erasmus the formal cause is matrimonial consent pure and simple rather than the somewhat mystical concord of sentiments and desires which Milton sées as part of the essential cause. The end of matrimony for Erasmus is propagation; Milton considers the end a concomitant of the formal cause and a consequent of it: the "best and sweetest purposes of marriage," its "cheif ends," he says, are *the helps and comforts of domestic life.*" Thus the marriage relationship for Milton becomes an end in itself rather than a means to a further end, the begetting and rearing of children. Children are a "necessity," as Milton says elsewhere,[31] but they are by no means part of the original design of marriage, which God instituted for the mutual comfort of husband and wife. In thus confining the causes of marriage to a personal relationship, a relationship which is self-enclosed except for its efficient cause, Milton severely breaks with varied authorities on the topic who saw the marriage relationship as extending far beyond that of mere husband and wife. Children, parents, commonwealth, church—Milton denies these any part in the essential marriage relationship. Continental and Puritan authorities who were disposed to deny the lawfulness of marriage without parental consent or to uphold the propagation and education of children in the interests of the civil or ecclesiastical body[32] as the primary end of marriage are implicitly controverted by Milton's disciplined but hardly conventional formulation of the nature of marriage.

For it is not accurate to assert that the primary end of matrimony according to the Puritans was the consolation of loneliness, "the grand object of matrimony—put first in Scripture

30. *Tetrachordon, CPW,* 2, 608–09, 612–13.

31. *Doctrine and Discipline of Divorce,* ed. Ernest Sirluck, *CPW,* 2, 235. This tract is hereafter cited as *D and D.*

32. See Johannes Polyandrus, A. Rivetus, A. Walaeus, and A. Thysius, *Synopsis Purioris Theologiae* (Lugdunus Batavorum, 1632), p. 756; William Perkins, *Christian Oeconomie,* p. 12; and Henry Smith, p. 23.

though third in the prayer book—which to the Puritan mind superseded and comprehended all others."[33] If the assertion were true, it would not be difficult to see Milton's definition and treatment of marriage as a logical outcome of a generalized "Puritan" attitude. But as a matter of fact there is evidence not only that the Puritans held otherwise, but also that there was little distinction between Puritan and Anglican on this point. Puritan preachers saw matrimonial ends in very much the same light as Anglican preachers. The objects presented were inevitably the same, with minor variations in the statement; they were derived from Scripture, Roman law, canon law, and the Book of Common Prayer. The objects were procreation, the avoidance of vice, and mutual solace. Procreation involved three aspects: the propagation of the human race; foundation of the family, upon which the state was based; and the spread of the church. William Gouge is especially lucid on this point:

> The *Ends* for which marriage was ordained, adde much to the honour thereof. They are especially three.
>
> 1. That the world might be increased: and not simply increased, but with a legitimate brood, and distinct families, which are the seminaries of cities and commonwealths. Yea also that in the world the Church by an holy seed might be preserued, and propagated, *Mal.* 2.15.
> 2. That men might auoid fornication (1 *Cor.* 7.2.) and possess their vessels in holinesse and honour. In regard of that pronenesse which is in mans corrupt nature to lust, this end addeth much to the honour of mariage. . . .
> 3. That man and wife might be a mutuall helpe one to another, (*Gen.* 2.18) An helpe as for bringing forth, so for bringing up children; and as for erecting, so for well governing their family. An helpe also for well ordering prosperity, and well bearing adversitie. An

33. William and Malleville Haller, "Puritan Art of Love," p. 245.

helpe in health and sicknesse. And [sic] helpe while
both live together and when one is by death taken from
the other.[34]

Other writers differ from Gouge only in citing other scriptural
passages, or in rearranging the order of the objects.[35] The second object is generally conceded to be a result of the Fall; yet
it is not any the less honorable for that.[36] The order in which
the objects are stated is usually the same as Gouge's and may
in some cases imply a hierarchy of ends. Milton will make much
of scriptural primacy in arguing for the primacy of the third
end (he cites Gen. 2:18), but that is a distinction proper to Milton's argument alone. Dod and Cleaver's allowance of marriage
between the old on the basis of the third end is, considering the
attitudes of other writers, even a shade liberal. The most significant feature of their statement of the third end, however,
is that personal affection is subordinated to domestic conven-

34. William Gouge, *Of Domesticall Duties* (2d ed. London, 1626), II, i, 24,
p. 122b.
35. See Perkins, *Christian Oeconomie*, pp. 13–14; Dod and Cleaver, *Household Government*, sig. K4^r–K5^r; John Donne, "Preached at a Mariage," in
Sermons, ed. George Potter and E. M. Simpson (Berkeley, 1952–58), *10*, Sermon 11, 244; William Herbert, *Herberts Careful Father and Pious Child*
(London, 1648), sig. X4^r; Robert Abbott, *A Christian Family Bvilded by God*
(London, 1653), p. 25; T[homas] H[ilder], *Conjugall Counsell* (London,
1653), p. 17; Matthew Poole, *Annotations upon the Holy Bible* (London,
1683–85), gloss on Matt. 19:10, sig. 1b. Two authors do not even mention
mutual solace as an end of marriage: John Wing, *The Crowne Conjugall*
(Middleburgh, 1620), p. 56, and William Secker, *A Wedding Ring Fit for
the Finger* (London, 1658), pp. 20–22. Although there is some disparity between Wing's incomplete statement of the ends of marriage and his subsequent discussion of the nature of matrimonial love, he says that the two
original ends of matrimony are "the *worlds multiplication*, & the *churches
propagation*. . . And . . . the *third*, (which came in *soe accidentally* by our
own corruption), [is] . . . to become a *remedy* and *cure* of our impure and
uncleane desires."
36. See John Calvin, *Institutes of the Christian Religion*, trans. Ford Lewis
Battles (Philadelphia, 1961), *1*, 406–07; *2*, 1257, 1484; Bartholemew Parsons,
Boaz and Ruth Blessed (Oxford, 1633), p. 17.

ience and household aid. "Solitarinesse" is essentially not a
state of mind demanding remedy, but a physical handicap.

Of those who clearly establish a hierarchy among the final
causes of marriage, the Anglican Jeremy Taylor is the most
perspicuous:

> The preservation of a family, the production of children, the
> avoiding fornication, the refreshment of our sorrows by the
> comforts of society; all these are fair ends of marriage and
> hallow the entrance: but in these there is a special order;
> society was the first designed, "It is not good for man to be
> alone";—children was the next, "Increase and multiply;"—
> but the avoiding fornication came in by the superfoetation
> of the evil accidents of the world. The first makes marriage
> delectable, the second necessary to the public, the third neces-
> sary to the particular . . . but of all these the noblest end is
> the multiplying of children.[37]

Taylor makes a distinction which Milton advantageously ignores: that there is a difference between temporal and essential
primacy. The fact that God's first intention in creating woman
was to provide a companion for man does not give this end
natural precedence over generation. Milton plays much upon
the phrase "prime institution of matrimony." Perhaps he ex-
ploits the ambiguity of chronological and hierarchical primacy;
but it is more likely that he sees the first biblical reference as an
indication of primacy of design. If so, Milton's interpretation
has a precedent not in Puritan writings on marriage but in the
rather more widespread literature of courtesy.

For Puritan and Reform writers tend to emphasize the same
final cause as Jeremy Taylor. Grotius sees marriage as necessi-
tated by the demands of legal identity and by the natural bond
between parent and child.[38] Most divines—both Puritan and

37. Jeremy Taylor, "The Marriage-Ring; or, the Mysteriousness and Duties of Marriage," *The Whole Works*, ed. Reginald Heber (London, 1822),
5, 258.

38. Hugo Grotius, *Discourses: 2: Of Christ, His Miracles and Doctrine*,
trans. and ed. C. Barksdale (2d ed. London, 1652), p. 61.

Anglican—consider the spread of the church through the begetting and education of children to be the primary function of marriage. The creation through marriage of a community of saints on earth to become the communion of saints in heaven is a theme which provides as much sermon material as the mystical marriage of Christ and the Church, or of the Lamb and the Virgin Soul. Both Anglicans such as Parsons and Donne and Puritans such as Perkins, Hieron, Bernard, Ames, and Needler give some emphasis to this objective, either as "the first and fairest end" (Parsons) of marriage or as the only proper motive to the begetting of children:

> The maine end and scope then that persons entring into this covenant of God, the mariage band must aime at, is that they may build Israel that out of their loynes may issue seed to be profitable mēbers of the church & cōmōwealth. for *hine coeli plantātur & etrrafundatur* [sic], out of marriage is heauen filled, & the earth established. . . . St. Paul requiring that *the yonger women should marry, beare children* I Tim. 5.4. maketh the end of marriage to be procreation and bearing of children.
>
> Parsons[39]

And yet in this second use [*in prolem*], we doe not so much consider generation as regeneration; not so much procreation as education, nor propagation as transplantation of children [into heaven].

> Donne[40]

Perkins at times recognizes only two ends of marriage: "Wedlock must be used to suppresse, then to satisfie that corrupt concupiscence of the flesh, & especially to enlarge the church of God. Rom. 13.14."[41] Both Hieron and Ames give special emphasis to the latter:

39. Parsons, pp. 29–30.
40. Donne, p. 245.
41. William Perkins, "A Golden Chaine," *Works* (Cambridge, 1603), p. 62, col. 2; see also "A Reformed Catholike," *Works*, p. 703, col. 2,

The rule of *seeking the kingdome of God first,* ought to take
place in all our undertakings, especially in Marriage, of
which the purpose in Gods ordaining it, is a *godly seed.* It is
the foundation of a family, and a family ought to bee a modell
of a Church; and therefore in it, that shold chiefly be intended, by which religion may be furthered.[42]

This conjunction is for the communication of bodies, because there is in marriage first sought an holy seed. Malac.
2,15.[43]

Bernard deplores the motives of people who desire children for
worldly reasons: "Most desire them for their name, for to pos-
sesse their inheritance after them, but not for the enlargement
of Gods Church."[44] And finally, Needler gives primacy to the
spread of the church among reasons for the creation of Eve.[45]
    The Anglican Bishop King and the Puritan Henry Smith use
an etymological argument to emphasize the primacy of procreation as the chief objective of marriage. Furthermore, this argument leads some writers to deny the name or the sanctity of
marriage to relationships in which children cannot be begotten:

The end of marriage is *proles,* issue. Therefore is it called
matrimonium, because they who are married *pater & mater
esse meditantur,* propose to themselves to become father and
mother.

                                                    King[46]

    42. Samuel Hieron, "The Bridegroome," in *Sermons* (London, 1614–20),
p. 469.
    43. William Ames, *The Marrow of Sacred Divinity* (London, 1642), p.
323.
    44. Richard Bernard, *Ruth's Recompence: or a Commentarie vpon the
Booke of Rvth* (London, 1628), p. 422.
    45. Benjamin Needler, *Expository Notes, with Practical Observations,
towards The opening of the five first Chapters of the first Book of Moses
called* Genesis (London, 1655), p. 50.
    46. John King, *Vitis Palatina* (London, 1614), p. 21.

the holy Ghost doth shew us three causes of this vnion.

One is the propagation of children, signified in that, when *Moses* saith, *He created them male and female:* not both male, nor both female, but one male and the other female; as if hee created them fit to propagate other. . . .

For this cause marriage is called Matrimony, which signifieth motherage, because it makes them mothers, which were virgins before. . . .

If children be such a chiefe end of marriage, then it seemes, that where there can be no hope of children, for age and other causes, there marriage is not so lawfull, because it is maimed of one of his ends, and seemes rather to be sought for wealth, or for lust, then for this blessing of children.

Smith[47]

this first and fairest end of marriage, procreation, is frustrated and evacuated by lust and lucre meeting together, either when an old silicernium . . . must yet marry with a young woman, or an old doting dame, *must have lust when she is old* . . . and be married to a young man in the flower of his youth. . . . Not to come together for procreation, is to wrong nature. Therefore nature to children doth not yet grant wives, to old persons it denieth marriage.

Parsons[48]

Support for Parsons' position is provided by Plutarch, Clement of Alexandria, Luther, and St. Augustine.[49] Even Erasmus, whom Milton admires for his frankness on the question of divorce, denies that marriage of the old is fitting, for the reason that procreation must be considered a primary element in the marriage bond. Perhaps the Puritan Richard Baxter, a near-contemporary of Milton's, most clearly shows the distinction which must be maintained, in any discussion of a "Puritan" idea of matrimony, between procreation as a universally recog-

47. Smith, *Sermons,* p. 13.
48. Parsons, pp. 35–36.
49. Ibid., p. 35.

nized end of marriage and the richly personal advantages of married life. The theme of matrimonial companionship receives rhetorical emphasis and is superbly articulated, but it never overshadows the conventional acknowledgment that matrimony was divinely instituted for the creation of new saints:

> As a married life hath its temptations and afflictions, so it hath its peculiar benefits, which you are thankfully to accept and acknowledge unto God. 1. It is a *mercy* in order to the propagating of a people on earth to love and honour their Creatour, and to serve God in the world and enjoy him for ever. It is no small mercy to be the Parents of a Godly seed: and this is the end of the institution of marriage, Mal. 2. 15. . . . 2. It is a mercy to have a faithful friend, that loveth you entirely, and is as true to you as your self, to whom you may open your mind and communicate your affairs, and who will be ready to strengthen you, and divide the cares and affairs and family with you, and help you to bear your burdens, and comfort you in your sorrows, and be the daily companion of your lives, and partaker of your joys and sorrows. 3. And it is a mercy to have so near a friend to be a helper to your soul; to joyn with you in prayer and other holy exercises; to watch over you and tell you of your sins and dangers, and to stir up in you the grace of God, and remember you of the life to come, and cheerfully accompany you in the ways of holiness. Prov. 9. 14.[50]

The view of marriage common to courtesy books of the same era allows for a wide range of possibility in discussions of the sentiments and emotions of the partners. As might be expected of books which deal with gentlemanly qualities, training, and conduct, the predominant concerns are secular. The reasons for marrying, as presented by the courtesy books, consist of two kinds: social or moral obligations and private advantages. Man has an obligation to marry for three reasons: to populate the earth by procreating and educating children, to serve the state,

50. Baxter, *Christian Directory,* p. 486.

and to control his lust. Of these three obligations, the first is usually mentioned or assumed, the second is most frequently given rhetorical development, but the third becomes less important, except in books which have a specifically religious cast. Earlier works, on the other hand, usually omit duty to the state as part of the formula. The *De Sponsalibus et Matrimonio* of Antonius Florentinus (Venice, 1474); the *Summa* of Johannes Andrea, and the *Silva Nuptialis* of Giovanni Nevizzano (Paris, 1521), distinguish two reasons for marriage: procreation and the avoidance of vice:

> Principalis tamen et prima causa est susceptio sobolis; propter hanc causam instituit deus matrimonium in Paradiso ante peccatum et inter primos parentes, quibus dixit: Crescite et multiplicamini. Secunda est vitatio fornicationis. Et ista causa habet locum post peccatum.

> However, the principal and first reason is the undertaking of a progeny; for this reason God instituted marriage in Paradise before the fall and between our first parents, to whom he said: Increase and multiply. The second reason is the avoidance of vice. And that reason had its place after the fall.[51]

Ariostos Seven Planets Governing Italie, a verse courtesy book translated into English in 1611, reiterates St. Paul's dictum that it is better to marry than to burn. Though the person himself is unmarried, he says:

> man cannot in perfect goodnesse stand
> vnless he live within the marriage band.[52]

But Ariosto considers the ill effects of fornication to have worldly as well as other-worldly consequences: in resorting to theft of the delights of marriage, man loses his "sense of love" and human kindness; indeed the worst offenders of all in their lack of charity are celibate but hardly spotless priests. Similarly,

51. Johannes Andrea, Cap. II, capitulum 4. See also Nevizzano, *Silua Nuptialis,* fol. xxiii, 1.
52. Lodovico Ariosto (London, 1611), p. 45.

The Glasse of Godly Love, a rather naïve and idealizing tract
whose range of quotation does not go beyond the Bible, enumer-
ates the following reasons for marriage: "most lovingly to helpe
and comfort one another, to bring forth children, and to in-
struct them in the lawes of God. Also, to auoyde Fornication
and all vncleanenesse."[53]
The difference between Ariosto's position and that of the
writer of this pious handbook is that Ariosto sees beyond the
divine prohibition to the social and personal effects of extra-
marital relationships. Ariosto's is a more sophisticated and secular though equally orthodox view. By the eighteenth century
the escape from the fires of lust is not even mentioned as a reason
for marriage: Mary Astell's *Some Reflections upon Marriage*
sees marriage as providing for "Domestick Quiet and Content,
and for the Education of Children."[54] But *proles* (issue) remained a significant function of marriage. Just as Alexander
Niccholes' *A Discourse of Marriage and Wiving* saw the begetting of offspring as the principal end of matrimony and slightly
discountenanced the marriages of those past the childbearing
years,[55] Mrs. Astell saw the rearing of children as a primary
duty. But she does not find it necessary, as Bacon, Niccholes,
and others do, to mention the biblical caution against burning
as an inducement to marry. The rationale for marriage had become progressively secular and commonsensical.
As John E. Mason says, the "prevailing tendency" of the courtesy books is to "regard [marriage] as a more or less unpleasant
duty to the state."[56] Bacon said in 1597: "Unmarried Men are
best Friends; best Masters; best Servants; but not always best
Subjects; For they are light to runne away; And almost all Fugi-
tives are of that Condition."[57] Thomas Fuller in 1642 also com-

53. (London, 1569), p. 179.
54. (London, 1700), p. 10.
55. (London, 1615), reprinted in *Harleian Miscellany*, 2 (1809), 158–59
and passim.
56. John E. Mason, *Gentlefolk in the Making* (Philadelphia, 1935), p. 245.
57. Francis Bacon, "Of Marriage and Single Life," *Essayes or Counsels
Civill and Morall*, ed. Israel Gollancz (London, 1901), p. 24.

mended the stability of the married man as an aid to the state
because of the loyalty that arises out of concern for his children:
"Though batchelours be the strongest stakes, married men are
the binders in the hedge of the Commonwealth."[58] For some,
like Francis Osborn (1656), who discommended marriage generally, it is only the state that reaps advantage from marriage;
he takes an almost Hobbesian point of view when he says that
for the individual "Marriage is a Clog fastened to the neck of
Liberty."[59] But others, like Richard Brathwait in *The English
Gentleman* (1641), point out that the state grants privileges to
the father of children: in ancient Rome, social precedence; in
Florence, exemption from taxes; in England, deferment from
military service "out of a tender respect to his posterity."[60]

The opposition between liberty and privilege leads into the
question of personal advantages and disadvantages of the married state. Some writers are eloquently specific about the disadvantages of marriage; others, like William Whately (1619), are
content with a generalized discouragement: "goe unto Matri-
monie with feare of the worst, and . . . know beforehand, that
there grow Briers and Thornes in this way, whereon he must
needs tread, that will travaile in it."[61] The disadvantages of
marriage most often mentioned are loss of liberty, diminishment
of wealth, the limitations imposed on action, quarreling between man and wife, the inferiority and vice of women, and the
troublesomeness of children.

The courtesy books tend to emphasize the secular social and
personal functions of matrimony in assigning final causes, but
in general they give no special prominence to mutual solace, to
matrimony *in adjutorium*. This is true partly because they are
concerned with marriage as a possibility rather than an accom-

58. Thomas Fuller, *The Holy State and the Profane State*, ed. Maximilian
G. Walten (New York, 1938), 2, 212.
59. Francis Osborn, *Advice to a Son* (8th ed. London, 1682 [1st ed. 1656]),
p. 33.
60. (London, 1641), p. 147.
61. William Whately, *A Care-Cloth* (London, 1624), sig. A4[r]. (The first
edition was published in 1619).

plished fact, with matrimonial choice rather than matrimonial obligations. Yet some of them make statements which are far more direct an anticipation of Milton's position than anything in the Puritan sermons and domestic conduct books. While the conventional reasons—to assuage loneliness or populate the earth—are usually mentioned, Ludovicus Vives, among other courtesy writers, argues from the nature of the institution that sexual commerce is subordinate to a spiritual affinity: "And in dede wedlocke was not ordeyned so muche for generacion, as for cetayne [sic] company of lyfe, and continuall felowshype. Neyther the name of husbande is a name of bodely pleasure, but of vnytee and affynytee."[62] This almost Platonic formulation of the ends of matrimony establishes a primacy for spiritual love which no Puritan writers are willing to concede. For the Puritan preacher, the primary function of marriage tends to exist apart from the means by which it is accomplished. A peaceable, mutually comforting relationship is the best means to accomplish the ends of matrimony, but it is in no way itself the main objective. For Vives, as for Milton, the spiritual bond establishes a reason for the legal bond.[63] For the usual Puritan writer, the spiritual relationship is a pleasing condition toward which the married partners work. It is not a preexistent epipsychical bond or a special moral predisposition. Furthermore, Puritan writers are not distinguished by any special concept of the relationship between husband and wife, as Haller and others seem to suppose. The emphasis upon the female as a help to her husband is as strong in Lady Dorothy Packington and Bishop Ussher as it is in any unquestionable Puritan, and Ussher lays the same stress

62. Ludovicus Vives, *The Instruction of a Christen Woman*, trans. Richard Hyrde (London, 1557), sig. Riii[r].
63. Vives is noteworthy for other reasons. There are many like him who account generation secondary among the causes of marriage, not because they consider the institution proper only to the husband and wife, but because they believe that procreation makes of the relationship a less spiritual one. See ibid., sig. AA3[v]–AA4[r]. See also Francesco Barbaro, *Directions for Love and Marriage* (London, 1677), p. 68.

upon mutual effort toward spiritual awakening.[64] The preacher who comes closest to Milton's position on the aims of marriage, Nathanael Hardy, is one whose sympathies are divided between Puritan and Anglican causes. He gives prominence to mutual help, both as the first reason for marriage, and as an index to the husband's proper attitude toward his wife:

> The wife since the fall is appointed for three ends, *ad remedium, ad sobolem, in adjutorium,* for a remedy against fornication, for the procreation of Children, and for helpfull communion; this last was no doubt the first in divine intention, and so ought to be in the mans apprehension. He that taketh a wife only as a remedy will love her but as men do physick, for use, yea, for meer necessity. He that marrieth onely for posterity will love her as a Mother not as a Wife. He onely can rightly love a Wife who looketh upon her, and accordingly taketh her for a yokefellow and companion: The right estimation then of a Wife is to account her as next to himself, and so above either children or servants.[65]

Milton's presentation of the objectives of matrimony in *The Doctrine and Discipline of Divorce* is remarkably different from that of the writers previously considered: "among Christian Writers touching matrimony, there be three chief ends

64. James Ussher, *A Body of Divinitie* (London, 1648), p. 106. Ussher, Archbishop of Armagh and Primate of Ireland, had been one of the supporters of episcopacy and the most learned and formidable apologist with whom Milton had had to deal in the antiprelatical tracts of 1641.

65. *Love and Fear: The Inseparable Twins of a Blest Matrimony* (London, 1653), p. 7. Hardy, at first a Presbyterian, became progressively loyalist and episcopal in his leanings. He preached many sermons on "The Royal Martyrdom" during the Interregnum, though without molestation from the government. He was apparently well liked by his Presbyterian congregation, who remained loyal to him. After the Restoration he became a chaplain to Charles II, and although he preached to a dissenting congregation throughout his middle and late career, it would be difficult to decide whether he was speaking as an Episcopal Puritan or as an Anglican. In any case, because of the taint of episcopacy, he could hardly be speaking as a Presbyterian.

thereof agreed on; Godly society, next civill, and thirdly, that of the mariage-bed."[66] These ends are arranged in the order of their importance. They seem to refer to religious companionship, social companionship (which is rather a redundancy; perhaps he means companionship on an everyday, human level—the society of ordinary speech, or mundane affairs as opposed to heavenly ones), and physical companionship.

Milton seems quite wrong concerning the agreement of "Christian Writers" on the ends of marriage he mentions. In his notes to the Yale edition of Milton's prose works, Ernest Sirluck makes no comment but quotes the Book of Common Prayer, Perkins, and Rivetus on the ends of marriage. None of them arranges the reasons for marriage in the same order as Milton, and their reasons are often different from his:

> 1. Book of Common Prayer: "procreacion [and rearing] of children," "remedye agaynste synne," "mutuall societie, helpe, and comforte."
>
> 2. Perkins: *Works, 3*, p. 671: Perkins expands the above to four ends by distinguishing between mere physical procreation and procreation of a church member.
>
> 3. Rivetus: *Theologicae & Scholasticae Exercitationes* (Leyden, 1633), p. 121: procreation, *vitae societas,* avoidance of sin.[67]

Milton sees and defines marriage quite apart from the social context in which most other writers view it; for him marriage is not essentially an institution preserving society from the chaos which would result if children should not have parents and if everyone should have sexual access to everyone else. He recognizes that the rearing of children is dependent on marriage,[68] but he defines it in personal terms: marriage satisfies a particular set of needs grounded in man's nature—the social needs of mind, affections, and appetites. Milton certainly derived his

---

66. *CPW*, 2, 268.
67. Ibid., n. 1.
68. *D and D, CPW* 2, 229–30.

formulation and ordering of the division of needs from Paraeus, though perhaps with some consciousness of Plato's theory of the tripartite soul:[69] the intellect has its needs (satisfied completely only by God but in marriage partly satisfied by the companionship of one who inspires piety or directs the mind to God); the affections have their needs (satisfied by human companionship); and the appetites have needs (satisfied by a household aid and a sexual object). Milton distinguishes among these ends in excellence, but also allows that each need must have its fulfillment: "if the particular of each person be consider'd, then of those three ends which God appointed, that to him is greatest which is most necessary: and marriage is then most brok'n to him, when he utterly wants the fruition of that which he most sought therein, whether it were religious, civill, or corporall society."[70] Each of these ends, then, is from the point of view of the *particular* person, a sufficient reason to marry; the frustration of any *one* of them, if he needs to have that end fulfilled, is sufficient cause for divorce.

Milton apparently considers procreation to be a function of the "society of the marriage-bed" or, at best, of civil society, and not a primary function of marriage at all. Since he reduces the significance of the social effects of marriage as not germane to the essential relationship, he ignores the question of what is to be done with the children of divorced parents[71] and minimizes the "weak supposes of Infants" as an issue in the ethics of divorce.[72] Children may affect the particular problem, but they cannot be made the basis of a general rule.

Milton's attitude toward the "society of the marriage-bed" in the divorce tracts is far from what we should expect of an author whose Latin poetry is Ovidian and from whom the unrefused connubial rites of Adam and Eve provoke a hymn in

69. Plato, *The Republic*, IV, 434D–441C. For Paraeus, see *CPW*, 2, 599, n. 35.

70. *D and D, CPW*, 2, 269.

71. See Axelrad, "One Gentle Stroking," pp. 92–104.

72. *Colasterion*, ed. Lowell W. Coolidge, *CPW*, 2, 734.

praise of matrimonial sexuality. The explanation lies partly in
the rhetorical situation of the tracts. Divorce for adultery and
desertion was readily allowed by Reform divines—though not
by English law;[73] such divorce was justified only on the grounds
of a violation of the agreement of bodily consent, of "benevolence" in the technical sense. In order to argue the necessity of
divorce in cases where other needs are unsatisfied, Milton must
stress their importance over that of bodily desire: in doing so,
he tends to diminish the force of physical anguish and the importance of physical society. The remedy of lust is a bland diet.
Since man is a rational creature, the form of marriage created
for him by God is essentially a rational delight, intended "to
satisfie that intellectuall and innocent desire which God himself kindl'd in man to be the bond of wedlock," and not "to
remedy a sublunary and bestial burning."[74] Essentially, this
is also the position of Milton in *Paradise Lost*. In the tracts,
Milton emphasizes the importance of "religious" and "civil"
society because divorce was not granted for the absence of
these, as it was granted for a violation of the physical bond.
Furthermore, the inability to perform the sexual act was universally recognized as an impediment to marriage. His opponents'
fallacious position in so allowing is derided by Milton in one
of his most cunningly extended periods:

> For although God in the first ordaining of marriage, taught us
> to what end he did it, in words expresly implying the apt and
> cheerfull conversation of man with woman, to comfort and
> refresh him against the evill of solitary life, not mentioning
> the purpose of generation till afterwards, as being but a sec-
> ondary end in dignity, though not in necessitie; yet now, if any
> two be but once handed in the Church, and have tasted in any
> sort the nuptiall bed, let them find themselves never so mis-
> tak'n in their dispositions through any error, concealment, or
> misadventure, that through their different tempers, thoughts,
> and constitutions, they can neither be to one another a rem-

73. Didbin and Healey, *English Church Law*, pp. 43, 78–79; Knappen,
Tudor Puritanism, p. 461.
74. *D and D, CPW*, 2, 269.

edy against loneliness, nor live in any union or contentment
all their dayes, yet they shall, so they be but found suitably
weapon'd to the lest possibilitie of sensuall enjoyment, be
made, spite of *antipathy* to fadge together, and combine as
they may to their unspeakable wearisomnes & despaire of all
sociable delight in the ordinance which God establisht to that
very end.[75]

Here, the accumulation of negatives, the climactic syntax ("For
although . . . yet now, if . . . yet . . .") and the interrupted verbal
construction, "they shall . . . be made," throw the weight of the
sentence on the contrast between the Greek derivative *antipathy*
and the homely neologism *fadge*, with its implications of clumsy
agreement and its dialectal overtones of slow, jogging movement. The helping verb and main verb are separated by an al-
lusion to the grounds of impotence and frigidity which stresses
by its position as well as by the grossness of the participle
"weapon'd" and by the emphatic negative "lest possibility" the
absurdity of the notion that copulation makes marriage. The
tension imposed by interruption and suspension gives rhetorical
prominence to the irritation of the speaker, the irrationality of
his opponents, and the unseemliness of the matches which law
uncritically inflicts upon human beings.

Milton's notion of marriage is not quite the same as Martin
Bucer's, although Milton discovered with pleasure that Bucer's
position was closer to his own than anyone else's. Like Milton,
Bucer believed that the purpose of marriage is to provide a
"meet help" for men, that true affection is an essential feature
of marriage, and that neither procreation nor *remedium forni-
cationis* forms the final cause of marriage, but rather "the
communicating of all duties, both divine and humane, each to
other, with utmost benevolence and affection."[76] The difference
between Bucer and Milton lies in the extent to which each is

75. *D and D, CPW*, 2, 235–36.
76. *The Judgement of Martin Bucer*, ed. Arnold Williams, *CPW*, 2, 456,
473, 465. This tract is hereafter cited as *Bucer*. All subsequent references to
D and D, Bucer, Tetrachordon, and *Colasterion* will cite the page number in
CPW, 2.

willing to define compatibility, and the methods which each uses to do so. Bucer takes matrimony wholly out of the context of the formal legal contract and makes it a bond dependent upon constant mutual agreement.[77] This constant agreement, an act of will, seems to represent the measure of marital concord. For Milton, on the other hand, matrimony is dependent upon a harmony of natures rather than will, a somewhat deeper bond over which the human being has little control. Aside from this distinction, however, which does not hold true in all contexts,[78] the agreement between Milton and Bucer is simply another indication of the divergence of Milton's own thinking from that of contemporary writers on marriage.

Milton's tractates on divorce are only in a very limited sense the distillation of a general "Puritan" ideal of marriage. It is true that most divines were conscious of the fact that marriage had many ends, so that there are occasional conflicts of opinion within the same writer. It is also true, as Haller notes, that Puritans promoted the ideal of a mutually helpful marriage. But on the whole, if one end was singled out as the major or prime end of matrimony it was never mutual solace. Milton's dependence upon this end as the basis of his argument has a certain daring which partly dooms the argument itself. For in arguing from the primacy of this end Milton truncates issues which needed to be explored. In isolating the personal aspects of matrimony and arguing from those only, he avoids social issues which were a large part of the consciousness of his audience. Furthermore, he gives philosophical formulation to a position which had been expressed openly though rather more informally by Bucer and Vives and which was not a characteristic feature of Puritan conduct books at all. Even Erasmus, whom Milton admired greatly, had not been willing so to argue the causes of matrimony. Honest and humane as Milton's formulation is, it is beyond the security of common assumptions, just as it is beyond the charge of mere philosophic restatement.

77. *Bucer*, pp. 445–46, 456.
78. See, for example, *Bucer*, p. 466, where "helples inabilitie" implies a potential natural defect.

2

Fitness:

The Conception of

the Ideal Mate

We are wrong in speaking of a bad choice in love,
since whenever there is a choice it can only be bad.

Marcel Proust, *The Sweet Cheat Gone*

Men may have chosen partners in marriage and in love no more
wisely in Milton's day than in Proust's, but seventeenth-century
matrimonial choice was always treated as though it could be subjected to a wholly rational standard. Courtesy books, conduct
books, sermons, tractates, and catechetical works reiterated
formulas which assured a fitting and proper choice. The ideal
mate, of course, had been created for Adam in Paradise, but
even she had proven fatal, and fallen man was obliged to pick
his way carefully through the grove of Eve's wayward daughters.
Reason had to teach and correct instinct, and handbooks of
matrimonial selection were meant to provide its cautionary
texts.

The choice of a mate apparently did not often devolve upon
parents. Some courtesy writers, like Vives, suggest that the parents should choose young men's wives because they are less
affected by their feelings ("more free from the agitations and
motions of al affections"). However, even Vives sees the danger
of such a system and advises against parents choosing a wife
merely on the basis of "honors," "power," "factions," or
"riches."[1] English writers, on the other hand, suggest strongly

1. Ludovicus Vives, *The Office and Duetie of an Husband,* trans. Thomas
Paynell (London, 1555), no signature.

that men seek advice but not rely solely on that. Niccholes uses
the proverbial caution about deliberation in marrying: "it is in
this action as in a stratagem of war: 'Wherein he that errs can
err but once,' " so that the man must use the "counsel of parents
and friends."[2] But he does not speak of allowing others to make
the final choice. Richard Brathwait suggests that parental decision in marriage can be abused and cause unhappiness: "what
miseries have ensued on enforced Marriages, there is no Age
but may record."[3] In general, the books dealing with matrimonial choice suggest that the right to make a bad choice of
partner is as inviolable as the right of individual conscience,
but that any man who wishes to make a wise choice should be
aware of the following considerations: age, rank, physical appearance, wealth, and moral character. The courtesy writer
often lavished his most telling *mots* on the discussion of choice.

Bacon says, and nearly every courtesy writer quotes him, that
men of any age can find an excuse to marry: "Wives are young
Mens Mistresses; Companions for Middle Age; and old Mens
Nurses. So as a Man may have Quarrell to marry, when he will."[4]
But one pitfall usually cited is too great a difference in ages:
those who marry older people expecting them to die soon "hang
themselves in hope that one will come out and cut the halter."[5]
On the other hand, the person who marries one much younger
than himself will find that he cannot match the energies of his
partner: "a difference in Age is a secret fire raked up for a time,
which will afterwards break out and consume your quiet."[6]

Advice upon the proper age for marriage was often specific
and frequently bizarre. Ralegh suggests that the best age for the
man to marry is toward thirty. Apparently the tendency which
the courtesy writers wished to check was that of marrying too
late. "Ever the young wife betrayeth the old husband, and she

2. *Discourse of Marriage*, p. 159.
3. *The English gentleman*, p. 145.
4. *Essayes*, p. 25.
5. Fuller, *The Holy State*, p. 214.
6. Archibald Campbell, Marquis of Argyle, *Instructions to a Son* (London, 1689), p. 46.

that hath thee not in thy flower, will despise thee in thy fall."[7] Another disadvantage of a late marriage is that the education of one's children falls to strangers and thus results in ill-bred progeny. And if one's early life is spent with harlots, one reaps the consequences of disease, waste of income, and the enmity of cast-off mistresses. On the other hand, people who marry too early are unfit to decide household matters and to manage a family.[8] Ariosto also supports thirty as the supremely marriageable age for the man, but for other reasons. At that age, the man should choose a wife of between eighteen and twenty: this disparity is recommended because there should be some correspondence between the woman's beauty and the man's potency:

a woman's glories ever faile,
Long ere the mans strength doe begin to quaile.[9]

Even twelve years' difference is not enough, because the woman's beauty will still falter before the man ceases to be attractive to her; but if he marries her at thirty, then he will be able to moderate his impatience and dislike when she does begin to offend his aesthetic sense, and so he will be able to tolerate her in his forties when she is a faded twenty-eight or -nine. The elaboration may not be offered in full seriousness, but the advice is.[10] How-

7. Walter Ralegh, *Advice to his Son: his Sons advice to his Father* (London, 1675), p. 87.
8. Ibid.
9. Ariosto, *Seven Planets*, p. 53.
10. Ibid. An even wider difference in age had classical authority. Women's reaction to the difference, which was all to the man's advantage, of course, was likely to be sharp. In Tilney's *The Flower of Friendshippe*, Master Pedro's discourse is interrupted by a sudden burst of feminine pique:
For *Aristotle* by hys reasons, would have the man to be twenty yeares elder than hys wyfe, bicause they might leave off procreation at one time. *Hesiodus* the Gréeke poet, & *Xenophon* the philosopher, would have the women fourteene, and the man thirtie yeres old, so that there should bée eyghtene yeres betwene them, bicause in that time, the man should be best able to rule his householde, and the woman taken from evill occasions. *Licurgus* lawe was amongst the *Lacedemonians*, that the men shoulde not marry, before thirtie, and seaven yeres of age, and women at

ever, even Ariosto is better able to countenance the marriage of
those too young than those too old.[11] According to Alexander
Niccholes, too, the young are better able to fulfill what he calls
the "right use of marriage"—the rearing of children—and the
old have difficulty finding partners: "Defer not thy marriage to
thy age; for a woman, out of her choice, seldom plucks a man
(as a rose) full blown." But he recognizes that young people seldom wait long enough: "if you ask when to marry they ['the
forward virgins of our age'] say: 'Fourteen is the best time of
their ages, if thirteen be not better than that.' "[12]

The advice given on the social rank of one's partner varies
from book to book. Most writers advise marrying a person of
similar status and wealth. Ariosto advises that one take a wife
suitable to one's "living and pedigree"; otherwise, if she is nobly
born and her mate is not, she will declare her need for two
pages, servingmen, gentlewomen servants, a dwarf, a fool, a
pander, a knave, dogs, monkeys, parrots, much company for
gaming, and a richly equipped coach.[13] Brathwait also advises
marrying a woman of equal rank to prevent bitterness in argument: "For I have seldome seene any difference greater, arising
from Marriage, than imparity of birth or descent, where the wife
will not sticke to twit her husband with her *Parentage,* and
brave him with repetition of her descent."[14] Niccholes suggests
marriage with someone of higher rank only if she also has an
income to maintain her style of living.[15] And Osborn advises his

---

eyghtene. What maner of equalitie is this quoth the Lady *Isabella,* I
would never marry, rather than to take such old crustes, whose wyfes are
more occupied in playstering, than in enioying any good conversation.
Master Pedro quickly agrees and goes on to reduce the recommended difference in ages to not more than five years. Edmund Tilney, *A brief and pleasant discourse of duties in Mariage, called the Flower of Friendshippe* (London, 1568), pp. 22–23.
11. Ariosto, p. 46.
12. Niccholes, pp. 163, 180.
13. Ariosto, p. 53.
14. Brathwait, p. 145.
15. Niccholes, p. 179.

son: "take one who thinks herself rather *beneath* than above you in Birth" since if she is an impoverished aristocrat, she will consume the young gentleman's riches.[16] But Argyle says the gentleman is to avoid above all marrying below him because the wife reacts with hatred and vindictiveness to the disgust toward him which such a marriage engenders.[17]

Courtesy books are full of advice as to the dangers of choosing a wife for her beauty; there are three special ill effects: (1) the attraction of beauty will fade, either because the man will tire of it or because the woman will grow old; (2) the woman's beauty will inspire designs in other men and cause her to be unfaithful; or (3) beauty will blind the man to other, more important considerations.

Beauty, of course, was not to be ignored as a value. To marry an ugly woman was to do disservice to oneself and one's children "for comeliness in Children is riches, if nothing else be left them."[18] Fuller says: "neither choose all, nor not at all for Beauty"; choosing for beauty alone, which decays, is like casting anchor on a floating island.[19] The dissatisfaction which follows the satiation of lust is mentioned by Ralegh,[20] and Osborn comments: "Other courses may weary us with Change, this with Continuance."[21]

The dangers of a beautiful wife are sobering. Osborn warns: "Make not a *celebrated beauty* the object of your choice; unless you are ambitious of rendering your house as populous as a Confectioner's shop; to which the gaudy Wasps, no less than the liquorish Flies, make it their business to resort, in hope of obtaining a lick of your Honey-pot."[22] Most writers make reference to the bias which beauty gives to choice, whether the bias is justified by other causes or not:

16. Osborn, *Advice to a Son,* p. 36.
17. Argyle, p. 44.
18. Ralegh, p. 85.
19. Fuller, p. 213.
20. Ralegh, p. 83.
21. Osborn, p. 33; see also pp. 28–29.
22. Ibid., pp. 29–30.

If she doe please you, then she vertuous is;
Nor any gift of goodness can she misse:
No Rhethoricke, reason, nor no strength of wit,
Can make thee loath when lust rules appetit.[23]

For these reasons the man is advised to seek a woman who is neither extremely beautiful nor extremely plain. Courtesy writers make few specific requirements, though Ariosto says the complexion should be smooth and light and the cheeks pink; high colors are a sign of an angry and peevish disposition.

The question of beauty allows those writers with a misogynist streak to satirize women for their artifice in dress. Osborn asks: Does beauty belong "to Nature, or the Dress?"[24] Both he and Ariosto[25] devote considerable sections of their works to a declaration of the fact that the beauty of most women is attributable to the efforts of hairdressers, dressmakers, shoemakers, and sellers of cosmetics.[26] Brathwait devotes two pages to the immorality of dyeing the hair, painting the face, and exposing the breasts, loading his guns with shot from Ambrose, Jerome, Tertullian, Cyprian, Clement of Alexandria, and Gregory Nazianzen, among others. He allows, grudgingly, that some defend the use of cosmetics when the woman's skin is blemished. But for the most part cosmetics tamper with the workmanship of God and therefore partake of blasphemy. Painting is "a reproving or reforming of the Almighty, whose workmanship is so absolute, as it admits of no correction."[27]

The importance of money as a motive shows up in all courtesy books on marriage. It is generally considered a greater desideratum than beauty, though not so important as virtue. Here differences in attitude occur if the writer happens to be a misogynist or an aristocrat. If he is a misogynist, he will place an exclusive value on money, as Osborn does: wealth is the best reason for marrying because other reasons are faulty; your wife's

23. Ariosto, p. 49; see also p. 52.
24. Osborn, p. 34.
25. Ariosto, pp. 54–56.
26. Osborn, p. 31.
27. Brathwait, pp. 143–44, 145.

noble birth implies that you will have to maintain large retinues and households for rank's sake, beauty is frail and subject to jealousy, and innocence can be slandered; only "a great Estate" will make you happy in marriage.[28] Osborn goes so far as to recommend that his son not trust to rumors about his fiancée's estate but investigate her financial condition personally. Argyle suggests that virtue is a primary qualification but money an equally necessary one: "Money is the sinew of Love, as well as War, you can do nothing happily in Wedlock without it; the others are Court-cards, but they are not of *the Trump Suit,* and are foiled by every sneaking misadventure; vertue is supprest . . . and beauty is betrayed to the necessity of keeping it so."[29] Argyle's witty comparison of virtue and beauty to cards which have a value in themselves and of money to cards which like trumps have an arbitrary value greater than that of kings, queens, and knaves—beauty and virtue—is a telling indication of the overwhelming value money can have for the courtesy writer, even though virtue is ostensibly valued higher.

Virtue is praised as a qualification for marriage by most courtesy writers for two reasons: (1) it is, like money, more permanent than beauty, and (2) it is less material and therefore of a worthier nature than either money or beauty. All writers, even Osborn, pay some lip service to virtue.

The wife's virtues were to include modesty, humility, patience, sobriety in dress, in drinking habits, and in conversation, obedience, and frugality. (The last is especially important to William Higford, who seems to have admired the "most excellent virtue Parsimony" above others.[30]) One could identify a virtuous woman by investigating her family, making inquiries of others about her disposition, and noticing her eye, walk, and behavior. If her eye roved and her walk was affected, she was more than likely to be lascivious. Even "women of low stature" were suspect.[31]

28. Osborn, p. 35.
29. Argyle, p. 43.
30. *Institutions or Advice to His Grandson* (London, 1658), p. 6.
31. Barbaro, *Love and Marriage* (London, 1677), p. 31.

In the later courtesy books there is a tendency to place less emphasis on virtue—not because it was less esteemed but because it was taken for granted as a desirable characteristic—and to place more emphasis on the woman's understanding and intellectual capacities. Earlier, Burghley and Ariosto had warned men that fools made bad wives, though Ariosto had also given cautions about witty women who could cover their tracks if they were unfaithful. But Mary Astell mentions the necessity of a "good Understanding" before that of a "Vertuous Mind" in the partner. She also mocks those who marry because they love someone's "Wit"—a qualification the earlier seventeenth-century writers had hardly thought it necessary to make.[32] The requirement that a woman be intelligent as well as virtuous indicates a slight shift in values and cultural roles at the beginning of the eighteenth century.

Divines, of course, tend to emphasize virtue as a basis of choice even more strongly than the courtesy writers. For them, the use of any other standard is perilous. Both Puritan and Anglican preachers comment frequently on the desirability and rarity of a virtuous woman[33] and advise close observation of the chosen partner before marriage to determine her moral disposition. Some writers declare that it is a sin to marry a woman for worldly reasons without considering "the better things."[34] Clerical writers counsel, in the choice of a partner, a purity of motive which will assure a satisfactory and lasting bond,[35] since virtue is no less than the binding force of matrimony.[36]

32. Astell, *Reflections upon Marriage*, p. 19.

33. For example, W. L., *The Incomparable Jewell* (London, 1632), p. 4: "Women, yee see, are sowed very thick, but vertuous women are reaped very thin, and are long a comming up, like Coteswold Barley."

34. Perkins, *Christian Oeconomie*, pp. 143–44.

35. See Thomas Taylor, *A Good Hvsband and A Good Wife* (London, 1625), p. 9: "All married persons must aboue all things, loue, respect and cherish grace one in another: ground not thy loue vpon beautie, riches, portion, youth, or such failing foundations: but pitch it first in God and grace, and it will hold."

36. See W. Crompton, *A Wedding-Ring* (London, 1632), p. 28: "looke first on vertue, and it is a marriage indeed, two made one by a mysticall vnion,

For Daniel Rogers, chastity, not love, is "the maine support of union, as the contrary is the chief dissolver of it," and for Richard Baxter choosing a wife for worldly reasons over "godliness" is a certain sign of reprobation.[37]

The case of the hapless lover who, mistaken in his choice, becomes bound to a bad wife, whether adulteress or shrew, provokes bitter animadversions as a caution to the imprudent. These denunciations and warnings are mostly derived from the proverbs of Solomon, whose expertise in matrimony was open to little question. Preachers did not hesitate to catalog the vicious wives of patriarchs from Adam on, and the story of Delilah was almost never omitted as a type of perfidy.[38] The greatest danger of an evil wife was that she was, by the nature of the marriage bond, close to the husband and therefore an incurable plague: "a more pestilent, pernicious, miserable, insufferable, evill, cannot (among temporall mischiefs) be imagined."[39] But a willingness to acknowledge the inherent dangers of a poor choice in marriage did not go beyond a caveat. It was never suggested that a lack of wifely virtue—unless manifested by adultery—could provide grounds for divorce. Matrimonial difficulties, however intense they might be, were to be met by prayer, forbearance, and an attempt to reform the offending partner.[40]

The kinds of virtue most admired in women were those which

---

representing that betweene *Christ* and his Church: the law may tye two together, that meet vpon sinister ends, vertue onely vnites them." Cf. Thomas Taylor, pp. 9–10: "When both are iust, grace will be cherished in each more then good nature: grace is excited by each in the exercise of spirituall duties; they pray with and for one another; they reade, conferre, and counsell together; they edifie one another on their holy faith, and this is a strong cement of loue."

37. Rogers, *Matrimonial Honovr*, p. 167; Baxter, *Christian Directory*, p. 484.

38. See *The Incomparable Jewell*, p. 4; John Wing, *The Crowne Conjugall* (Middelburgh, 1620), p. 34.

39. Wing, p. 32.

40. Herbert, *Careful Father and Pious Child*, sig. W2ᵛ–W3ᵛ. See also Henry Hammond, *A Practical Catechisme* (London, 1646), pp. 80–83.

would not merely lessen the danger of infidelity but aid in the management of a household. Housewifery was the "womans trade":

> It is no shame or staine therefore for a woman to be house-wifely, be she neuer so well borne, be she neuer so wealthy. For it is the *womans trade* so to be; it is the *end* of her *creation;* it is that that she was made for. She was made for man, and given to man, not to be *a play-fellow,* or *a bed-fellow,* or *a table-mate,* onely with him, (and yet to be all these too,) but to be *a yoake-fellow, a worke-fellow, a fellow-labourer* with him, to be *an assistant* and *an helper* vnto him, in the manag-ing of such *domesticall* and *household affaires.*[41]

To contest or usurp the husband's authority was acknowledged to be the gravest household sin, and therefore the passive vir-tues—obedience, peaceableness, meekness, patience, and silence —were generally the most highly prized and the most often com-mended to prospective husbands.[42] Loyalty, chastity, and sobri-ety were other essential virtues. And the more active virtue of frugality proved the woman's bent for domestic economy. But the humility of the woman was her chief commendation: *"A kinde and a courteous disposition is a thing much to be respected in the choyce of a wife. A meeke and a quiet spirit, in a woman* especially, *is a thing,* saith *Saint Peter, much set by in Gods sight.* And the one commonly followeth and accompanieth the other."[43] But Milton was to turn the emphasis upon feminine passivity to good advantage as an argument to demonstrate the possibility of erroneous choice. Silence, after all, was an ambigu-ous quality. It might indicate a submissive nature; it might also indicate intellectual dullness.

The difficulty of finding a virtuous woman and of maintain-

41. Thomas Gataker, *A Marriage-Prayer* (London, 1624), p. 19.
42. See Robert Wilkinson, *The Merchant Royall* (London, 1615), sig. D2^r–D3^r. Secker holds that the perfect choice was the woman who would "be subject to your dominion," "sympathize with you in your affliction," and "be serviceable to your salvation" *(Wedding Ring,* pp. 53–54).
43. Gataker, p. 19.

ing a peaceful household was not underestimated by either secular or religious authors. The pessimism of Francis Osborn was
matched by that of William Whately, Thomas Fuller, and the
author of *The Incomparable Jewell.* Consciousness of the importance of the right choice was strong in all writers on marriage. Cautions in choosing a mate could, however, be reduced
to one principle, whether we name it appropriateness, equality,
or "fitness."

The reader of the courtesy books was advised to choose a
compatible mate, suited to his temperament and occupation;
if the family was noble, he was to try to marry a collaterally related family and strengthen the nation's institutions and moral
standards by avoiding divorce; he was to make sure that his prospective wife loved him; he was to remember that marriage was
permanent; he was not to expect marriage to be free from all
inconveniences; and he was to be mindful of the weak nature
of women and the possibility of shrewishness and infidelity.

On the question of suitability, the wife was to be compatible
in humor and mood, and she was to conform to the traditions of
the husband's household, especially the size of his retinue and
servant force.[44] Alexander Niccholes is emphatic on compatibility: the joining of liberality with miserliness, of "heroical
thoughts" with "dull affections," of "knowledge with ignorance
where there is no zeal to communicate; [of] old age with youth,
where there is no desire of enjoyment" he finds a dangerous
foundation for marriage. The choleric man should choose a
meek wife, the rake should "smell . . . out a wife a little tainted,"
the traveling merchant should choose a patient wife "lest otherwise, thou abroad, she prove an actor with thy factor at home."[45]

The Marquis of Argyle advises "cross marriages between Families"—a controlled inbreeding so long as the marriages do not
occur within the degree of kinship which weakened the Haps-
burgs.[46] Love was more difficult to regulate. However, the
reader could tell whether a woman loved him by her interest

44. Ariosto, p. 51.
45. Niccholes, p. 165.
46. Argyle, p. 44.

in preserving his estate—i.e. by her frugality—and her desire to
please him in conversation without his having instructed her
to do so. The question of the preservation of love in marriage
is a topic to which the courtesy books give much attention. But
Fuller warns that marriage "is not like the hill Olympus, ὅλος
λαμωρὸς, wholly clear, without clouds; yea, expect both wind
& storms sometimes, which when blown over, the aire is the
clearer, and wholsomer for it."[47]

The question of fitness was usually handled in a slightly different way by divines, whether Puritan or Anglican. "Fitness"
was understood in two senses, likeness of nature and appropriateness of character, breeding, and social conditions. Perkins
distinguishes kinds of fitness for marriage, depending on
whether the "signs" are "essential" or "accidental" to the contract. The essential marks are opposition of sexes, nonconsan-
guinity, ability to perform intercourse, freedom from contagious
disease, and freedom from any previous marriage contract. The
principal accidental marks are similarity of religion, equality
of age and status, and the good reputation of both parties to the
contract.[48] Whately usually uses the term "fit" in the sense of
essential fitness, although he too will use it in the wider sense.[49]
The distinction between the meanings of the term is crucial,
because upon it depends the author's interpretation of the divine intention in creating marriage: "I will make him a fit help"
—or "a help meet for him."

47. Fuller, p. 213.
48. Perkins, *Christian Oeconomie*, pp. 23, 24, 54, 55, 57, 59, 62. William
Secker uses "fitness" and "meetness" in reference to woman's human nature,
as opposed to the nature of angels or beasts, with whom Adam could not
mate. But he also uses the terms to designate the qualities in the wife which
ought to correspond to those of the husband—qualities of temperament,
rank, and faith ("the Harmony of her disposition," "the Herauldry of her
condition," "the holiness of her Religion"—pp. 43–47).
49. Cf. Whately, *A Care-Cloth*, pp. 28, 71. Robert Abbott enlarges Perkins'
"essential" marks of fitness but uses the term "fit" to refer only to them,
rather than to the "accidental" marks: "[marriage] is for all *fit couples:*
fit I say, because not for men and men, women and women, men and beasts,
Christians and Infidels: for we must not be *unequally yoked*" (*Christian
Family*, pp. 25–26).

William Gouge interprets the phrase in a way significantly
different from Milton. Like Abbott and Whately, he uses it essentially as an instruction to avoid bestiality, homosexuality,
incest, bigamy, and polygamy. It bears, secondarily, upon personal and emotional characteristics, but these do not affect the
nature of matrimony: "Thy [sic] who have power to mary must
be carefull in chusing *an helpe meet for them:* for this was
Gods care when first he instituted marriage. To make an helpe
meet for marriage, some things are absolutely necessary for the
very essence or being of mariage: others necessary for the comfort and happiness of mariage."[50]

In Milton, Gouge's second category ("things . . . necessary
for the comfort and happiness of marriage") is given equal importance with the first. But preachers differed over the qualities
noted as conducive to matrimonial comfort. Some, like Gouge,
restate conditions which resemble those designated by most
courtesy writers: "That matrimoniall society may prove comfortable, it is requisite that there should bee some equality
betwixt the parties that are maried in *Age Estate, Condition,
Piety.*"[51] The "equality" Gouge speaks of, like "similitude," or
"parity," or "fitness" in the broader sense, is obviously a variable
which does not negate the contract of marriage but does affect
the relationship which the parties to the contract will create:

> In similitudine uero spectatur aequalitas. Quanq̄ potest in-
> cidere similitudo, inter quos non est aequalitas: rursus
> aequalitas, inter quos non est similitudo. . . . Quū opibus,
> aetate, genere, forma pares coëūt, pariter et similitudo adest &
> aequalitas. [Similitude, indeed, tends toward equality. How-
> ever, similitude can occur among those who share no equality:
> conversely, equality can occur among those who share no
> similitude. When equals in riches, age, birth, and beauty
> conjoin, both similitude and equality are present in the same
> degree.]
>
>   Erasmus[52]

50. Gouge, *Of Domesticall Duties,* p. 107b.
51. Ibid., p. 109b.
52. Erasmus, *Matrimonii Institutio,* sig. S1ᵛ.

but in truth many mēs daughters may goe out and bewaile
the daies of their marriage, yea and many men too look back
to the single life . . . and so are they punished with late repentance. . . . And what is the cause of this? lack of forecast,
because they found not first whether it be fit to marry, or yet to
marry, or whether he be fit, or she be fit, fit in degre, in disposition, in religion.

                                                        Wilkinson[53]

Discussions of ideal matrimonial affinity often either explicate
or cite the passage in Genesis, "*Faciamus adiutorium simile
sui*"; one example is Bishop King's discussion of the mutuality
of the relationship:

The woman at her first creation was made to bee a *sicut*. *Sicut*
is of similitude, so is a woman. Look back to the first institution, *Faciamus adiutorium*. . . . Of what quality? *Simile sui*,
like to himselfe: There is the *sicut*. *Simile?* what is that? . . .
Simile sui, that which is *contra ipsum*, not contrary; but *è
regione*, face to face, as the Angels stood over the mercy-seat;
coram ipso, as a glasse that reflecteth and returneth upon a
man his owne image, that is, *quasi alter ipse, ipse coram ipse*,
an other selfe, him selfe before himselfe. Or *simile*, that is,
secundùm, iuxta, penes, propè, proximè, ad manum, the next
of all others, and at hand to minister unto him whatsoeuer is
wanting. This is that *sicut*, which I speake of. A *sicut* in
mutuall loue, in naturall affection, in the communion of woe,
(for they are σύξυγοι, yoke-fellowes; and must remember that
bonum coniugium, sed à iugo tractum, in marriage is an yoke)
in the participation of good things, in society of offices, in coniugall faith, indissoluble couenant, (that is *particeps foederis*)
in parity of religion. They must be συγκληρονόμει τῆς χάριτος,
coheires of the same grace.[54]

53. Wilkinson, *Merchant Royall*, sig. Cʳ–Cᵛ.
54. King, *Vitis Palatina*, pp. 10–12. The image of the two angels facing
one another over the mercy seat as a metaphor for mutual piety in marriage
is also used by William Secker, p. 30.

In this passage Bishop King defines the spiritual likeness of woman to man in terms of metaphoric physical attitudes: the seraphic vis-à-vis, the reflected mirror image, and the proximate figure. Such attitudes suggest an equivalence and balance of spiritual power which emphasize the full sharing of feelings and duties. The human bond is created by a parity of emotional and physical effort. The fact that King's sermon was preached at the marriage of an English princess to the Prince of the Palatinate may account for some of the emphasis on parity, but it is also true that this sermon, like others of its kind, was published as a guide to conduct for all married couples. King, like other divines and the courtesy writers, locates the sources of matrimonial unity in love, sympathy, sorrow, common participation and mutual duty, fidelity, the legal contract, and religious faith. The contract then establishes by law a bond which is emotional, physical, and moral as well. The man searching for a wife is to keep all these aspects in mind to assure himself of a proper "likeness," and religion is, of all of them, "the sweetest and strongest tie."

King's emphasis upon a natural disposition to love and upon religious similarity is expressed somewhat differently by John Donne, who minimizes the likenesses to which the courtesy books[55] had devoted so much time but who isolates personal and emotional characteristics even more clearly than King as the foundation of the marriage-bond: "I will make thee a help like thy self: not always like in complexion, nor like in years, nor like in fortune, nor like in birth, but like in minde, like in disposition, like in the love of God, and of one another, or else there is no helper."[56] Donne here goes beyond the usual understanding of the passage as referring to a generically similar mate; the mutual "disposition" and love "of one another" suggest a particular affinity between man and woman and not merely the likeness of kind. Furthermore, Donne's strong "or else there

55. Typing, *The Fathers Covnsell* (London, 1644), p. 21; cf. King, pp. 14–15.
56. Donne, *Sermons,* p. 247.

is no helper" implies that emotional correspondence is a necessity of the institution of marriage itself. Donne never gives this
idea a formal demonstration, but the implied primacy of spiritual likeness imparts a special meaning to the biblical phrase.
Thomas Taylor adopts a position similar to Donne's, but he
formulates it as a series of moral imperatives to the wife:

> The wife must frame herself in all lawful things to helpful-
> nesse, to shew the likenesse of her minde to his minde, of
> her will to his will, of her affections and manners to his, as
> therein also to acknowledge the end of her Creation, next the
> service of her Creatour, to be every way helpful unto man.
> A wife, as a wife, is to no end, but to frame her selfe to her
> husbands minde and manners; so as to stand in a contrary
> minde, and to crosse his will, his speeches, his lawful desires,
> and commands, on which God hath stamped his image, is to
> cast off Gods image and ordinance, and misse the end of being
> a wife.[57]

The difference between Taylor and Donne is partly rhetorical;
one is writing a sermon, the other a catechism. But Taylor
demonstrates precisely how in the individual case fitness became fact, and how marriage involved a dynamic adjustment
not so much on the part of the husband as on that of the wife.
Choice was a matter of masculine judgment; concord, of feminine pliability. Taylor is not merely dealing with matrimonial
quarrels; he is establishing a system of behavior (based on
natural differences)[58] by which God's purposes can be fulfilled.
The feminine virtue of humility was essential to the creation of
a suitable relationship.

57. *Certain Catechistical Exercises Treating of the Grounds of Religion,*
pp. 1–168 in *Works,* ed. Edm. Calamy, A. Jackson, S. Ash, et al. (London,
1653), p. 154.
58. Ibid., p. 153: "all the parts of Gods image were more cleare in *Adam*
then in *Eve;* and the woman was then the weaker vessel, as the Serpent
knew. And as the left hand hath the same soul, head and spirits, and is a
needful help to the right; yet the right hand is the stronger."

Furthermore, Taylor's words show clearly how the focus of "purpose" in marriage can be shifted from the institution to the individual. If marriage has its ends, being a husband and being a wife also have theirs. And therefore the whole issue of "fitness" can provide a vocabulary for redefining marriage as a relationship of woman to man rather than as a social, moral, or legal phenomenon. Hence it is not a Puritan emphasis upon *vitae societas* as a prime function of matrimony—an emphasis which clearly does not exist—but rather the moral importance given to psychological attunement, chiefly a duty of the wife, which furnishes Milton with some of his arguments and definitions.

The importance of the term "fitness" in Milton's argument can be estimated by the fact that he made "love born of fitness" the formal cause of marriage. Put another way, fitness is that condition which makes love possible; and it is important for the understanding of Milton's argument to recognize that the condition is dependent on two factors: the individual essence and the human will. Some human beings are suitable to one another by nature, others are radically unsuitable; of those suitable, some render themselves "unmeet" for another through perversity of will and behavior.[59] Since God's institution of matrimony was a promise to create a "help meet" for man, marriage cannot exist where unfitness exists, whether this unfitness is a defect of nature—understood as *individual* nature—or of will. Milton makes of God's promise to Adam a promise to all mankind that his matrimonial partner shall meet the requirements of his mind and spirit. Unlike most of his Puritan contemporaries Milton consistently interprets the phrase *"adiutorium simile sui"* so that the likeness of personal disposition takes precedence over the likeness of kind. Whether Milton is determining the way in which God can be said to join human be-

---

59. Milton occasionally distinguishes opposition of nature from willful contrariety; in these cases the term "unfitness" applies to the unwilled rather than willed defect. (See *Colasterion*, p. 723, where "perversenes" does not seem to include "apparent unfitnes.")

ings or defining his use of the term "wife,"[60] the phrase "meet
help" has reference to similarities of individual temperament,
emotional response, and intellect, rather than to the mere
generic likeness of man and woman. *Individual* fitness is the
essential criterion of marriage as part of the divine plan.

Since Milton's tracts deal with defective rather than sound
marriage, we can understand his concept of the ideal condition
only by an examination of the negative term "unfitness." Milton
eventually equates unfitness with all of the causes for which
divorce was allowed in the Old and New Testaments, with the
Old Testament causes of "uncleanness" and "hatred" in *The
Doctrine and Discipline of Divorce* (pp. 244, 306), and with the
New Testament cause of "fornication" in *Tetrachordon* (pp.
671–73). The source of unfitness is some defect or imperfection
in one of the parties to the contract which may manifest itself in
open adultery but in any case renders married life intolerable.
The fault is usually referred to the wife. Milton's argument, like
Bucer's, depends on the fact that to the extent that the wife is
no meet help she is no wife, and the marriage itself will have
been null and void to the extent that it cannot have occurred in
the first place by virtue of the wife's defect; otherwise, if God
promised meet help and yet gave none to man—indeed, forced
him to remain married to a wife who could not fulfill her duty—
He would be guilty of a contradiction. Since God cannot con-
tradict Himself, those who seek to make Him do so by inter-
preting His law as permanent matrimony when there is no
matrimony are guilty of arrant blasphemy.[61]

The most extensive delineation of unfitness occurs in
Tetrachordon, where Milton matches Bucer's audacity by defining fornication as a violation of the intention of God in
creating matrimony, hence, as "a constant alienation and disaffection of mind, or . . . the continual practise of disobedience
and crossnes from the duties of love and peace, that is in summ,
when to be a tolerable wife is either naturally not in their power,

60. *D and D*, pp. 328, 309; *Tetrachordon,* pp. 603–670.
61. *Bucer,* pp. 473, 474.

or obstinatly not in their will" (p. 673). By the qualifiers "constant," "continual," "naturally," and "obstinatly," Milton apparently seeks to forestall the objection which was in fact put forward by his opponents and answered with scorn in *Colasterion*—that the condition of unfitness was alterable. Milton in fact says nothing in this respect of willful contrariety, but his opponents' suggestion that temperament is a matter of physic and of diet calls forth one of the coarsest somatic analogies in Milton: "to my freinds, of which may fewest bee so unhappy, I have a remedy, as they know, more wise and manly to prescribe: but for his freinds and followers . . . I send them by his advice to sit upon the stool and strain, till their cross dispositions and contrarieties of minde shall change to a better correspondence and to a quicker apprehension of common sense, and thir own good" (pp. 737–38). Correspondence of temperament, like the individual constitution itself, is not wholly amenable to human effort. To emphasize the fact that human nature is capable of special forms of affection for certain human beings but not for others, Milton relates his concept of nature to those medieval allegories of Dame Fortune, whose symbols were drawn from a commonplace astrological system:

> For Nature hath her *Zodiac* also, keepes her great annual circuit over human things as truly as the Sun and Planets in the firmament; hath her *anomalies,* hath her obliquities in ascensions and declinations, accesses and recesses, as blamelesly as they in heaven. And sitting in her planetary Orb with two rains in each hand, one strait, the other loos, tempers the cours of minds as well as bodies to several conjunctions and oppositions, freindly, or unfreindly aspects, consenting oftest with reason, but never contrary.[62]

The key word in the first sentence is "blamelesly," as in the second it is "reason." Nature affects human beings according to the laws which governed the creation of the world; these principles in themselves are "reason," and reason is the faculty by

62. *Tetrachordon,* pp. 680–81.

which man discovers them. There is, however, an implied margin of irregularity in which reason in man either cannot predict or cannot understand nature's movements; there is an area in which man can only see that her choice does not violate the larger framework in which he operates. By this analogy with astronomical hypotheses, Milton explains the fact that some human beings are unfit for others as marriage partners; as the movements of the stars are subject to the control of natural laws, so the relationships between human beings are subject to natural affections which reason cannot always chart. The "anomalies" and "obliquities" of human response are, according to Milton, in some cases impossible to control. And for these eccentricities both nature and man must be held blameless. The concept of a nature which adjudicates the emotional correspondence between human beings gives to "fitness" and "unfitness" the status of law, the sanction of an inner reason, and the immutability of nature itself.

The fact that certain emotional characteristics are unchangeable allows Milton an answer to the charge that his thesis made possible "divorce at pleasure." Divorce was possible only between those who were initially unfit to marry each other; those who were fit were truly married and would so remain. Divorce in Milton's sense of the term is to be understood as the legal manifestation of a state which has always existed internally in the parties to the contract of marriage. Only those who divorce "violently," "conspiringly," or "rashly" commit adultery by their separation;[63] and there is a sense in which the paradox of Algernon Moncrieff, "Divorces are made in heaven," sums up Milton's position with a curious exactitude. In fact, Milton gives to divorce the honor consistent with the divinely ordained process of nature itself. For, since unfitness is a natural and immutable defect, and since conjugal love is dependent upon fit-

63. Ibid., p. 669. There is a curious parallel to Milton's theory of affinities in the English translation of a German mystical treatise entitled *A Spiritual Journey of a Young Man* (London, 1659): "when God's essential Spirit, neither makes nor joynes the marriage together, then it is not any marriage in his holy Spirit" (p. 98).

ness, the presence of unfitness is an essential barrier to the possibility of "true" marriage. As an essential rather than accidental defect, it is more evil than adultery, for which the Bible amply allows divorce.[64] The condition of unfitness, as Milton refers to it, is obviously a spiritual condition; it is an unfitness of mind equivalent to "uncleanness."[65] But as a spiritual condition, it has physical effects: it not only induces hatred and prevents the possibility of love or concord, but also creates physical displeasure, dissolves the union of bodies as well as minds, and reduces matrimony to the level of bestial intercourse.[66] Yet the condition is by no means mutual; as Milton defines the term, it is clear that he intends it to apply to the wife alone. The most extensive discussion of the term "fornication," in *Tetrachordon,* accords with the notion already evident in Thomas Taylor and John Donne that matrimonial harmony depends largely upon the wife's adjustment to her role, her duties, and her husband's domestic comfort. "Uncleanness" is "a constant alienation and disaffection of mind," "the continual practise of disobedience and crossnes from the duties of love and peace," and "a perpetuall unmeetnes and unwillingnesse to all the duties of helpe, of love and tranquillity" (pp. 673–74).[67] The result is that "in this general unfitness or alienation she can be nothing to him that can please. In adultery nothing is given from the husband, which he misses, or enjoyes the less, as it may be suttly giv'n: but this unfitness defrauds him of the whole contentment which is sought in wedloc" (p. 674). The precedence given by Milton

64. *D and D,* pp. 332–33.
65. Ibid., pp. 244, 306.
66. *Colasterion,* pp. 733, 731, 747, 733.
67. The widening of the meaning of the term "fornication" among the Jewish theologians is discussed by Henry Hammond in *A Paraphrase and Annotations Upon all the Books of the New Testament* (2d ed. London, 1659), p. 30. Hammond evidently did not subscribe to the enlargement. In *A Practical Catechisme,* he upholds by means of subtle, refined, and highly unconvincing arguments the notion that adultery is the only legitimate ground for divorce.

to male authority and male judgment in divorce is sanctioned by St. Paul's interpretation of the verses of creation: God created man in his own image, whereas woman "is not primarily and immediately the image of God, but in reference to the man" (p. 589). Hence the usual (though by no means universal) case is that the man exceeds the woman in intellectual capacities, and, therefore, "seeing woman was purposely made for man, and he her head, it cannot stand before the breath of this divine utterance, that man the portraiture of God, joyning to himself for his intended good and solace an inferiour sexe, should so becom her thrall, whose wilfulness or inability to be a wife frustrates the occasionall end of her creation [i.e. the end for which she was created], but that he may acquitt himself to freedom by his naturall birthright, and that indeleble character of priority which God crown'd him with" (pp. 589–90). Milton nowhere suggests that the wife may plead the "unfitness" of the husband as a cause for divorce. She may divorce him for other reasons, such as adultery or heresy (p. 591), but "unfitness" is a defect proper only to the wife.

While it is not surprising that Milton carries into his argument the same rhetoric of denunciation which the clergy had used against relationships which they felt violated the natural order, he regards as unlawful what the ordinary divine would have considered merely inappropriate or unfortunate. As a result, he not only declares the primacy of unfitness over adultery and frigidity as a cause for divorce but also uses terms similar to those in which lawless marriage was condemned: "what can be a fouler incongruity, a greater violence to the reverend secret of nature, then to force a mixture of minds that cannot unite, & to sowe the furrow of mans nativity with seed of two incoherent and uncombining dispositions?"[68] The suggestion that such a marriage is *contra naturam* seems a daring application of the "law of nature."[69] For nature is here to be understood

68. *D and D*, p. 270.

69. For a full discussion of this term, see Sirluck, ed., *CPW*, 2, 145–58, especially 154–58, and Axelrad, "One Gentle Stroking," pp. 24–26, 45–59. See also Perkins, *Christian Oeconomie*, p. 162.

as the temperament of a single human being, raised to the status
of a valid law. Elsewhere, notably in his discussion of the Old
Testament laws,[70] Milton consistently equates the divine intention implied by the Mosaic divorce law with a true understanding of the condition of man after the Fall. With respect
to all moral issues—including that of divorce—Milton finds
the law of nature, the law of the Old Testament, and the law of
the Gospel essentially the same.[71] There can be no inconsistency among these, since they are all the work of God himself and all are summed up in the "law of Christ"—the law of
charity. The frequency with which the word "charity" is used
in the divorce tracts has been noted by others, (e.g. Axelrad,
Sirluck), but it has not been noted that charity is equivalent to
divine universal law, or that this law is founded upon human
well-being: "the great and almost only commandment of the
Gospel, is to command nothing against the good of man, and
much more no civil command, against his civil good."[72] Milton
is nowhere so conscious of the human measure of all law as in
the divorce tracts.

But this is, of course, only to declare that the prohibition
against divorce is not merely an unreasonable discomfort to
mankind, but a direct offense against the whole law and finally
against God himself, an act of blasphemy: "if it be unlawful for
man to put asunder that which God hath joyn'd, let man take
heede it be not detestable to joyne that by compulsion which
God hath put assunder."[73] For Milton sees true marriage as a
final expression of the divine harmony inherent in the composi-
tion of things, the capstone of the universal order. If it results in
concord and serenity, marriage is the work of God, a fulfillment
of the divine plan; if it arouses discord it is a frustration of
that plan and the work of the devil. By giving the theory of
elemental magnetism—of unity through love and chaos through
hatred—psychological equivalents in matrimony, Milton is able

70. *D and D,* p. 354.
71. *Tetrachordon,* pp. 636, 640.
72. *Tetrachordon,* pp. 638–39.
73. Ibid., p. 651.

to make some rather interesting moral equations. The whole issue of fitness becomes a profoundly ethical one. The association of divinity and harmony, on the one hand, and diabolism and enmity, on the other, inevitably implies that to seek to make permanent a marriage relationship in which strife is constant is to do the devil's work:

> there is indeed a twofold Seminary or stock in nature, from whence are deriv'd the issues of love and hatred distinctly flowing through the whole masse of created things, and . . . Gods doing ever is to bring the due likenesses and harmonies of his workes together, except when out of two contraries met to their own destruction, he moulds a third existence, and . . . it is error, or some evil Angel which either blindly or maliciously hath drawn together in two persons ill imbark't in wedlock the sleeping discords and enmities of nature lull'd on purpose with some false bait, that they may wake to agony and strife, later then prevention could have wisht.[74]

The ultimate conclusion of such a theory is that a marriage between enemies violates the principles of natural sympathy and offends against God in His most profound and essential role of Creator; the passage in the 1644 version of the *Doctrine and Discipline of Divorce* contains a significant phrase which Milton is to repeat in the prologue of *Paradise Lost* and which suggests the creative power inherent in the disjunction of antipathies: "by his divorcing command the world first rose out of Chaos, nor can be renew'd again out of confusion but by the separating of unmeet consorts." Only thus, by applying the recognized moral values of harmony, creation, and nature to the very process of divorce, and by using the analogies of elemental attraction, astronomical conjunction, and divine demarcation not merely as analogies but as other manifestations of the same natural principle, can Milton give to "fitness" as he defines it the quality and resonance of a moral absolute.

The mortal institution of matrimony, like other institutions,

74. *D and D,* p. 272.

should reflect the ideal order of nature. When a marriage differs from the "true" marriage of fit partners, it is a travesty of natural love, engendering repulsion rather than sympathy. Milton considers the human institution both accidental and mutable, partaking of the character of absolute law only when it reflects some spiritual reality: "if Mariage be but an ordain'd relation, as it seems not more, it cannot take place above the prime dictats of nature; and if it bee of natural right, yet it must yeeld to that which is more natural, and before it by eldership and precedence in nature."[75] The corollaries of Milton's position are that as an "ordained relation," the bond can be broken, that no civil covenant should be allowed to ruin man, and that, although it is dependent on a civil ruling, a marriage may be void ipso facto.[76] Since God does not join unlike things, the sense in which "union" can be applied to some marriages is metaphorical and relative only.[77] And since divorce may be necessary to preserve a higher order, God intends divorce, and man sins in not allowing it.[78] The ultimate paradox of Milton's position, a paradox dependent on the careful discrimination between "true" and merely civil marriage, is that not to allow divorce is to dishonor the institution of marriage itself.[79]

Milton's discussions of matrimonial choice, like those of the courtesy books, stress difficulties of judgment. But unlike the courtesy writers, Milton deals only with questions of temperament (rather than age, beauty, wealth, and virtue), and his position, of course, implies that a choice once badly made ought not to be irrevocable. He also emphasizes the lack of experience and the heavy consequences such a choice necessarily involves; some "have unwarily in a thing they never practiz'd before, made themselves the bondmen of a luckles and helples matrimony."[80] It is, in fact, the psychological and social probability

75. *Tetrachordon*, p. 621.
76. Ibid., pp. 621, 623; *Colasterion*, pp. 750, 741.
77. *Tetrachordon*, pp. 666–67.
78. Ibid., p. 682; *D and D*, p. 310; *Tetrachordon*, p. 651.
79. *D and D*, p. 253.
80. Ibid., p. 240.

of a bad choice which provides Milton with his most cogent
arguments for the injustice of universal permanence in marriage: those who have practiced continence have not the knowledge of those whose "wild affections unsetling at will, have been
as so many divorces to teach them experience"; one cannot,
within the bounds of customary access, learn enough to make a
proper choice; the pressures and assurances of friends may precipitate a rash confidence about suspected incompatibility; and
eagerness to marry may cloud the judgment. One final argument is that the meekness so prized by the courtesy writer may
be a snare: "who knows not that the bashfull mutenes of a virgin
may oft-times hide all the unlivelines & naturall sloth which is
really unfit for conversation."[81]

It is apparent, then, that although Milton may have borrowed
his rhetoric, his attitudes, and his arguments from courtesy writers and divines, he by no means used exactly the same concept of
matrimonial compatibility. His concept of fitness differs from
that of the courtesy writers in having no bearing at all upon the
characteristic concerns of material or moral status. It differs
from that of the divines in having less to do either with sexual
appropriateness or religious similarity and in being both less
and more "religious" than that of the divines from whom he
adopted it. It is less religious in being less specifically concerned
than they that the married partners belong to the same sect.
(Milton does not use "fit" or "fitness" in reference to the mere
similarity of religious convictions, even though he discusses this
similarity as essential.) But it is more religious in that Milton
is aware of the implications for their religious life of the marriage of unfit partners. Furthermore, Milton's concept goes beyond the usual definition of compatibility. Milton's ideal of the
similarity of temper reflects certain Platonic assumptions; it is,
for instance, far more dependent than that of either the cour-
tesy-book writer or the preacher on a theory of soul relationships, divorced from most considerations of bodily or religious
"fitness." It seems to have reference to a preordained universal

81. Ibid., pp. 249–50.

order whose rule extends into private relationships as deeply as into the social and cosmic framework.

For Milton's conception of matrimony as a harmony of souls and wills is a direct result of his conviction of universal order. The musical analogy of concord[82] is not the only means by which Milton characterizes the operation of the divine will in marriage. Order might be restored to the institution of matrimony by divorce "which like a divine touch in one moment heals all; and like the word of God, in one instant hushes outrageous tempests into a sudden stilnesse and peacefull calm."[83] The associations of health and serenity with the divorce of "unmeet" couples is not accidental. True marriage in Milton is an emblem of natural order, just as, to the divines, it was an emblem of the authority of Christ over the church. And although the human institution of marriage violated the order of nature, the possibility of its amendment gave man the opportunity to create a reflection of that order, to follow in his laws as closely as possible the internal dispositions of things.

82. Cf. such phrases as "true concord" (D and D, p. 330), "all civil and religious concord, which is the inward essence of wedlock," "discordant weldoc" (Tetrachordon, pp. 605, 666), and "the unchangeable discord of som natures" (Colasterion, p. 717).
83. D and D, p. 333.

3

Conversation:

The "Aptitude of Variety"

"In Arcady, when you go, you'll find the food is vile."

Ronald Firbank, *Inclinations*

Milton's characterization of marriage as a "meet and happy conversation"[1] may be misunderstood by the modern reader, to whom the word "conversation" usually denotes talk. Milton's usage is that of the prayer book. He did not conceive of marriage in quite the same way as Nietzsche did—"Do you believe that you will be able to converse well with this woman into your old age?"[2]—nor for him would the ideal woman have been Lou Salomé. "Conversation" meant, rather, association, living with, companionship, society. It would include talk to the extent that association required it, but it need not have included a great deal of correspondence or communication on intellectual matters. The defect which Milton most decries in marriage is an emotional, not as intellectual, one (although he does not express such a dichotomy). It is her failure to perform the "acts of peace and love" which makes a woman's society displeasing and "fit conversation" impossible.

Milton's references to matrimonial conversation in the divorce tracts generally associate the ideas of love, peace, lightheartedness, and mutual comfort; they also give precedence to the demands of the spirit over those of the body. As the "soul"

1. *D and D*, p. 246.
2. Friedrich Nietzsche, *Human, All-Too-Human* (New York, 1954), 406, p. 59.

of the marriage relationship,[3] conversation should provide precisely those conditions that satisfy the ends of marriage, which Milton in *Tetrachordon* arranges hierarchically: "in matrimony there must be first a mutuall help to piety, next to civill fellowship of love and amity, then to generation, so to household affairs, lastly the remedy of incontinence" (p. 599).

Nicholas Byfield, among others, made "quietness" as well as "love" a necessity of happy marriage,[4] but in Milton peace, more than a desideratum, becomes the essential condition of wedlock, and the word recurs in the divorce tracts with considerable frequency and emphasis. Marriage is made for man's good and peace;[5] man seeks in marriage "the obtainment of love or quietnes";[6] the "main end of marriage" is "peace and comfort," "conversing solace and peaceful society," and the "peace and contentment of mans mind";[7] the "main benefits of conjugall society" are "solace and peace";[8] the "inward essence of wedlock" is all civil and religious concord,[9] as peace is the essence of the matrimonial conversation;[10] and unmeetness renders "solace and peacefull society" impossible.[11] Although Milton does not so specify, it can be presumed that peace was in the special domain of the woman; the tradition of the shrew does not seem distant from these reiterations, and matrimonial writers make peace a particular duty of the wife, since it is the nature of women to be vexatious.[12]

But women also provide men with a very special kind of emotional and intellectual pleasure. Milton distinguishes between

3. *D and D*, p. 276.
4. *A Commentary: or, Sermons vpon the Second Chapter of the First Epistle of St. Peter* (London, 1623), p. 713.
5. *Colasterion*, p. 733.
6. Ibid., p. 755.
7. *Tetrachordon*, p. 623.
8. *D and D*, p. 242.
9. *Tetrachordon*, p. 605.
10. *Colasterion*, p. 739.
11. *D and D*, p. 244.
12. Vives, *Christen Woman*, sig. Yii^v–Yiii^v.

friendship and conjugal love by characterizing the former as
"grave" and the latter as "amiable and attractive." He is careful
to indicate that he is not merely referring to the sensual delights
of matrimony, but rather to a kind of amorous gaiety that distinguishes one's behavior with a woman:

> there is one society of grave freindship, and another amiable
> and attractive society of conjugal love, besides the deed of pro-
> creation, which of it self soon cloies, and is despis'd, unless it
> bee cherisht and reincited with a pleasing conversation.[13]

God intends this "free and lightsom conversation" in marriage
as a solace for pensive man; and conversation ideally is "cheer-
full and agreeable," fulfilling the personal end of marriage, "delight in the society of another."[14] The wife helps to restore to
her husband by her society a less burdensome habit of thought;
she should be an "intimate and speaking help, a ready and re-
viving associate in marriage."[15] Marriage is ultimately a spiritual recreation for man, and the relationship between the wife
and the husband is akin to that between Wisdom and God:

> No mortall nature can endure either in the actions of Re-
> ligicn, or study of wisdome, without sometime slackning the
> cords of intense thought and labour: which lest we should
> think faulty, God himself conceals us not his own recreations
> before the world was built; *I was*, saith the eternall wisdome,
> *dayly his delight, playing alwayes before him*. And to him
> indeed wisdom is as a high towr of pleasure, but to us a steep
> hill, and we toyling ever about the bottom: he executes with
> ease the exploits of his omnipotence, as easie as with us it is to
> will: but no worthy enterprise can be don by us without con-
> tinuall plodding and wearisomnes to our faint and sensitive
> abilities. We cannot therefore alwayes be contemplative, or
> pragmaticall abroad, but have need of som delightfull inter-
> missions, wherein the enlarg'd soul may leav off a while her

13. *Colasterion,* p. 740.
14. *D and D,* pp. 273, 248, 235.
15. Ibid., p. 251.

severe schooling; and like a glad youth in wandring vacancy, may keep her hollidaies to joy and harmles pastime: which as she cannot well doe without company, so in no company so well as where the different sexe in most resembling unlikenes, and most unlike resemblance cannot but please best and be pleas'd in the aptitude of that variety.[16]

Milton will again use the phrase "prime ends of marriage" in reference to mutual solace and help.[17] Marriage is a help to bear life's afflictions, "a league of love and willingnes."[18] Marriage consists in performance, not speech; and, since Eve was Adam's rib, love and help are the sinews by which the wife, "a comfortable helpe and society," demonstrates her kinship with her husband.[19] This demonstration is the only binding force of matrimony; marriage is indissoluble only so long as it is helpful to man by curing loneliness.[20] If helpful, marriage will produce the contentment necessary to its nature.[21]

Milton's emphasis upon the emotional and spiritual realities of marriage is an attempt to counteract the narrower views responsible for British law. But even the English reformers generally thought of marriage in physical terms; for them adultery, the violation of the physical unity of marriage, was the only legitimate cause of divorce between believers.[22] Both Perkins and Ames allow no other causes than infidelity and idolatry as disruptions of the marriage bond[23] and adultery as the only specific offense against it. Perkins employs the term conversation only in reference to pure or adulterous physical association.[24] Grotius, on the other hand, maintains that the tie of bodies is

16. *Tetrachordon,* pp. 596–97.

17. Ibid., p. 601.

18. *D and D,* p. 311; *Tetrachordon,* p. 624.

19. *Colasterion,* p. 750; *Tetrachordon,* pp. 670, 604.

20. *Tetrachordon,* pp. 594–95, 605; *D and D,* p. 309.

21. *D and D,* pp. 331, 270.

22. Didbin and Healey, *English Church Law,* pp. 44, 45.

23. Perkins, *Christian Oeconomie,* pp. 62, 119; Ames, *Marrow,* p. 325.

24. *Christian Oeconomie,* pp. 67, 80: e.g. "unclean and unchast conversation" of the Israelites.

dependent on the tie of affections; he argues that both the union of bodies and the entire bestowal of affection are essential to marriage but he gives precedence to the latter.[25] Among Puritan clerics, William Whately uses the term conversation with consciousness of both social and sexual meanings.[26] But only Milton makes so insistent a plea for the fundamental primacy of the spiritual bond in matrimony.

Milton defines the contract as a marriage of minds "fitly dispos'd" rather than of bodies.[27] In fact, a marriage which is merely physical is no marriage; "conjunction" is to be understood as relating to the mind rather than the body; and conversation is as essential to matrimony as bodily conjunction.[28] Conversation is essentially the solace of human loneliness, a solace which answers a peculiarly human need. The perfection of Eve as a consort was dependent on her *spiritual* fitness for Adam; having placed man above the beasts in the order of nature, it was mandatory that God create a woman, not merely in order to provide a generative instrument for man but to satisfy his longing for a creature who was responsive to his spiritual nature. It is basically in this sense that Eve was a "meet help"; not in the sense that she was female. Milton expresses this necessity of spiritual companionship in various ways throughout the tracts. Loneliness is said to need a "compliable mind" and "unity of disposition."[29] Meetness consists of the "effectuall conformity of disposition and affection." The "mind" should be "answerable" to the body in matrimony; otherwise man is more than alone: "God cannot in the justice of his own promise and institution so unexpectedly mock us by forcing that upon us as the remedy of solitude, which wraps us in a misery worse than any wildernes."[30] Milton defines matrimonial conversation as

25. Grotius, *Discourses*, pp. 61–62.
26. *A Bride-Bush* (London, 1617), p. 6.
27. *D and D*, p. 328.
28. *Tetrachordon*, pp. 598, 611; *D and D*, pp. 239–40.
29. *Tetrachordon*, pp. 602–03, 650; *D and D*, p. 326.
30. *Tetrachordon*, pp. 600, 598.

companionship, as true friendship and familiarity;[31] and he heaps abuse upon his opponents who cannot conceive of conversation in any but physical terms.[32] An "unconversing inability of minde" (or heart) is said to be opposed to the "purest and most sacred end of matrimony."[33]

Milton emphasizes spiritual rapport so heavily because he defines marriage by specifically human needs. The humanity of marriage depends on its being a spiritual society, as does its dignity.[34] Milton's concept of sex is informed by the same humanism, the awareness that human sexuality is not merely a matter of physical compatibility. The delight of the body is dependent upon the delight of the mind; the mere act of sex debases or causes despair where there is no "souls union and commixture of intellectual delight."[35] Milton goes so far as to give the "burning" of which St. Paul speaks a spiritual meaning—an interpretation which has no exegetical support. Marriage alone satisfies this "rationall burning,"[36] but only a marriage based upon mutual spiritual likeness. Where this likeness does not exist to produce the appropriate "conversation," then the condition of the marriage is best defined as tyranny:

> What is this, besides tyranny, but to turn nature upside down, to make both religion, and the minde of man wait upon the slavish errands of the body, and not the body to follow either the sanctity, or the sovranty of the mind unspeakably wrong'd, and with all equity complaining?[37]

Matrimonial conversation, then, was capable of being variously understood. It might refer only to simple intimacy, mere living together,[38] but it might also refer to the mutual perform-

31. Ibid., p. 682.
32. *Colasterion*, pp. 742, 747.
33. *D and D*, p. 248.
34. Ibid., pp. 275, 252.
35. Ibid., pp. 246, 339.
36. Ibid., p. 251 and n.
37. *Tetrachordon*, pp. 599–600. Cf. *Tetrachordon*, p. 692; *Colasterion*, p. 732.
38. Samuel Hieron, *Sermons*, p. 406.

ance of religious duties.[39] It might even include a very special kind of moral and intellectual refreshment, most clearly illustrated in the charming picture of matrimonial nurture given by Vives:

> For the wyfe shoulde couple and bynde hyr husband unto hir every daye more and more wyth hyr pleasant and gentyl condicions. For nothyng dothe more drawe and entice unto it, than doth pleasant condicions and swete speche. A wyse woman shuld have in minde mery tales, & historyes (how be it yet honest) wherwith she maie refreshe hir husband, and make him mery, when he is wery. And also shee shall learne preceptes of wysedome, to exhort him unto vertue or draw him from vice and all, and some sage sentences againste the assaultes and rages of both fortunes, both to plucke downe hir husbandes stomacke, if he be proude of prosperitee and wealth: and to comforte and courage him, if he be striken in heavinesse with adversite.[40]

These "pleasant condicions" and "swete speche," along with a joyful piety, seem to be what Milton requires in the conversation of a "help meet" for man. For Milton, the concerns of piety and affection precede those of the body,[41] and the mind (of the woman) is the source of peace and love.[42] Furthermore, Milton, like Vives, considers moderation in physical intercourse to be an expression of man's celestial nature. As Vives puts it:

> For these holy folkes understoode well enoughe, that thyng which is written of wise men, that the bodily pleasure is unwoorthy this excellent nature of ours, which wee haue of the soule. And therefore every bodye dispiseth it the more and casteth it away, the more that he hath of that excellencie of

---

39. Thomas Taylor, *A Good Hvsband and A Good Wife*, pp. 9–10.

40. *Christen Woman*, sig. AA^r–AA^v. John Shaw's funeral elegy attributes to his wife some of these skills (John Shaw, *Mistris Shawes Tomb-stone* [London, 1658], pp. 28–29).

41. *Tetrachordon*, p. 599.

42. *D and D*, p. 248.

the soule, and the nigher that he is to God and other heavenly mindes, neither will use this pleasure often, excepte it be suche as have but beastelye, vile, and abiecte mindes. And have taken muche of vyle nature, and very littell of that highe and celestiall nature.[43]

The term "love" is used by most marriage writers in two different, though related, ways. The first use of it grows out of St. Paul's dictum, "Husbands, love your wives" (Colossians 3:19). The term therefore can refer to a special duty of the husband, identifying the precise manner in which he should regard his wife. This aspect of love will be taken up under the respective duties of the married partners. The second use of the term, however, refers to the relationship itself and to the common duties of both partners. For some writers, marriage is by definition *coniugium*, a "joyning of hearts"; love is said to be "essential" to it, but the absence of love does not violate the contract, uncomfortable as the married partners may be:

> To shew the loue which should be betweene man and wife, Marriage is called *Coniugium*, which signifieth a knitting or ioyning together: shewing, that vnlesse there be a ioyning of harts, and a knitting of affections together, it is not marriage indeed, but in shew and name, and they shall dwell in a house like two poysons in a stomake, and one shall euer be sicke of another.[44]

This love is referred to as the essential strength and music of marriage,[45] but there was no attempt to see an invalidation of the contract in prolonged contention:

> As God hath ordained remedies for euery disease, so he hath ordained a remedy for the disease of marriage. The dis-

43. *Christien Woman*, sig. AA3ᵛ–AA4ʳ. This passage follows one page of examples of moderate use of the marriage bed: Zenobia (who allowed her husband to touch her only for procreation), Ethelffrida (who refused to sleep with her husband after bearing one child), Edethrudus (who imposed chastity on herself and two husbands), and assorted conjugal celibates.

44. Smith, *Sermons*, pp. 27–28.

45. Ibid., p. 27.

ease of marriage is adultery, and the medicine hereof is di-
uorcement. *Moses* licensed them to depart for hardnes of
heart; but Christ licenseth them to depart for no cause but
adultery. If they might be separated for discord, some would
make a commoditie of strife; but now they are not best to be
contentions [sic], for this law will hold their noses together,
till wearinesse make them leaue struggling; like two Spaniels
which are coupled in a chaine, at last they learne to goe together, because they may not go asunder. As nothing might
part friends, but *if thine eye offend thee pull it out;* that is,
if thy friend be a tempter: so nothing may dissolue marriage,
but fornication, which is the breach of mariage; for marriage
is ordained to auoide fornication, and therefore if the condition be broken, the obligation is void.[46]

Milton alone sets forth the contradiction implied in this view
of marriage. His solution is the paradox that marriage is least
violated by him who continues in peace and love, whether this
be in marriage or in divorce. Divorce, in other words, preserves
love, the essence of marriage, better than marriages forcibly continued by law.[47]

Conjugal love is, among the writers on marriage, invariably
defined as love of a particular sort; it is one of three kinds of
love which men owe to others, depending on their mutual relationship:

> *Spirituall* Love is that we bear to a woman as she is a
> Christian, and so where there are the greatest measures of
> grace, there ought to be greater degrees of love; and in this
> respect another woman may deserve love when a mans own
> wife doth not, because she may want those impressions of
> grace which others have: Naturall love is to a woman as
> woman, and thus a man may love other women besides his
> wife, but still he must love his wife before other women;
> Matrimonial Love is of the wife as she is a wife, and this is
> solely and wholly due from every man to his own wife: The

46. Ibid., p. 45.
47. *D and D,* p. 258.

Greek word ἀγαπᾶν here used signifieth as much as ἀγὰν παίειν . . . such a love whereby a man rests satisfied in the object loved.[48]

Discussions of the nature of conjugal love tend to treat it as an expression of the individual self, or of the special powers of human beings, or of the principle of correspondence in nature. The quality of conjugal love is like self-love: it is "cordial" (heartfelt), "constant," "tender," "industrious" (manifesting itself in labor directed toward the welfare of the love object), "pure," and "superlative."[49] Since it is an intensification of a normal relationship among human beings, its mark is greater charity, along with faithfulness and helpfulness. It is, in fact, precisely an outgrowth of those considerations which predetermine a proper choice—*spiritual* considerations—and it therefore necessarily involves contentment and satisfaction with one's choice of a marriage partner for one who maintains his spiritual values.[50] These attitudes all tend to give to conjugal love the paradoxical quality of a selfless expression of what is best and most spiritual in oneself.

The emphasis given to matrimonial affection as a particularly intense kind of spiritual, yet human, attachment[51] informs Milton's attitude toward marriage as the crown of human relationships. Furthermore, since in the hierarchy of love conjugal love is next to spiritual love, its importance is plain.[52] This spiritual importance is further underscored by the analogy frequently used to characterize married love—the love of Christ for his Church.

Finally, conjugal love summed up for the Renaissance the secret of cosmic order. Asking the source of love was a popular Elizabethan riddle which often had no answer.[53] All that

48. Hardy *Love and Fear*, p. 12.
49. Ibid., pp. 14–17.
50. Whately, *Bride-Bush*, pp. 6–8.
51. See Wing, *Crowne Conjugall*, pp. 31–32.
52. Ibid., pp. 43–46; also Bullinger, *Christian Matrimony*, fol. 4ʳ.
53. See George Pettie, "Icilius and Virginia," *A Petite Pallace of Pettie His Pleasure* (Oxford, 1938; London, 1576), p. 103.

could be said was that love was the process which mysteriously
united people's natures.[54] Without leaning heavily on the
Neoplatonic correspondences or Platonic theories of love,
clergymen could point to the unity of married life as an example
of the universal law of unity in division.[55] In general, they did
not attempt to account for love; but they did emphasize its
likeness to the love of God, its properly spiritual basis, and its
resemblance to the unity of natural things. The clergy was
careful to point out that love was a necessity in all things, not
just in marriage, and that conjugal love answered to a very
special order of being.[56] For Milton, of course, such love was
the essence of marriage:

> the material cause of matrimony is man and woman; the
> Author and efficient, God and their consent, the internal
> *Form* and the soul of this relation, is conjugal love arising
> from a mutual fitnes to the final causes of wedlock, help and
> society in Religious, Civil, and Domestic conversation, which
> includes as an inferior end the fulfilling of natural desire, and
> specifical increase; these are the final causes both moving the
> efficient, and perfeting the *form*. And although copulation be
> consider'd among the ends of marriage, yet the act therof in
> a right esteem can no longer be matrimonial, then it is an
> effect of conjugal love.[57]

As charity was considered to be the fulfillment of the law, so
love was considered the sum of all duties in marriage.[58] To
Jeremy Taylor it was the quintessence of many virtues and con-
tentments.[59] It manifested itself in both benevolence and affection, as well as in the more specific duties of married life.
"Benevolence" included a wide spectrum of meaning. Among

54. Pettie, "Sinorix and Camma," *Petite Pallace*, p. 12.
55. See Hardy, p. 3.
56. John Preston, *The Breast-Plate of Faith and Love* (3d ed. London,
1632), 3, 20; Rogers, *Matrimoniall Honovr*, p. 150.
57. *Tetrachordon*, pp. 608–09.
58. See Gouge, *Domesticall Duties*, p. 132a.
59. *Works*, p. 269.

many of the early courtesy and matrimonial writers, it referred
to the yielding of the body to the marriage partner.[60] However,
Vives defines the term as a more comprehensive feeling than a
willed physical surrender:

> [ea beneuolentia] transit ad nurus, generos, affines, propin-
> quos unde maximae saepe amicitiae ac cōciliationes sunt
> natae, et fundatae civitates [that benevolence passes to
> daughters-in-law, sons-in-law, relatives by marriage, and kins-
> men, whence often the greatest friendships and alliances are
> created and cities founded.][61]

Among the later writers, "benevolence" refers either to the
proper attitude toward the duties of marriage[62] or to the
general desire for another's welfare.[63] Nathanael Hardy makes
a traditional distinction between *amor benevolentiae* and *amor
complacentiae;* he considers the latter, satisfaction in the enjoyment of another, more proper to matrimonial love.[64] Perkins gives the fullest explanation of "benevolence" in *Christian
Oeconomie,* where it has three applications: the use of the body,
mutual cherishing (preservation), and mutual solace and joy
(the love and kindness which Perkins considers seemlier in the
young than in the old).[65] The sexual overtones of the term are,
however, never lost. Milton rarely uses the word except to refer

---

60. Bullinger, fol. 26ʳ⁻ᵛ; Ames, *Marrow,* 2, xix, 40, p. 323. This meaning
survived in popular usage. See *The Humble Petition of Many Thousands
of Wives and Matrons of the City of London and other parts of this Kingdome* . . . (London, 1643), p. 6, and Henry Nevile, *The Ladies Parliament*
(London, 1647), A1ʳ. The term also occurs in Moses à Vauts, *The Husband's
Authority Unvail'd* (London, 1650), p. 94. Hammond, in *Paraphrase of the
New Testament,* glosses the word as the wife's due in marriage, and includes under it physical companionship and the husband's love, honor, and
"kindness" (pp. 531–32).
61. Vives, *De Officio Mariti* (Basileae, 1540), p. 7. Cf. Erasmus, *Christiani
Matrimonii Institutio,* sig. O7ʳ.
62. Ussher, *Body of Divinity,* p. 287; Smith, p. 16.
63. Hardy, p. 8.
64. Ibid.
65. Pp. 111–23.

to the yielding of the body;[66] where he wishes to refer to other matrimonial obligations, he uses the term "conjugal duty." At times, however, even in Milton, "benevolence" has the force of a mental disposition which has physical effects.[67] In any case, Milton considers the physical duty a violation of the soul if it is performed only out of compulsion.[68] Done without love, and only under the restraint of law, it cannot be considered a human act. Other matrimonial writers concur in speaking of benevolence; the sexual act is proper only if performed cheerfully, holily, and seasonably.[69] And Milton speaks of loving with "that sincere affection that marriage requires."[70]

The reiterated analogy between human marriage and the relationship between Christ and his Church best exemplifies the complexity of the concept of married love. For Dod and Cleaver, the analogy demonstrates the special concern of the male for the female, the affection which causes him to cherish and nourish her as his own body.[71] For Crompton, it refers to the virtuousness of their married union.[72] For Gouge, it expresses the authority of male over female.[73] For Bucer, it summarizes the matrimonial duties of honor and obedience on the one hand and love and cherishing on the other.[74] And for Milton, the analogy identifies for man the intensely personal love—not merely "civil" love—which the institution of marriage should reflect.[75]

66. See *Tetrachordon*, pp. 692, 701, 708.

67. See *D and D*, p. 270.

68. *Tetrachordon*, pp. 625–26.

69. Whately, *Bride-Bush*, pp. 43–44.

70. *Tetrachordon*, p. 669.

71. *Household Government*, sig. F8ʳ.

72. *Wedding-Ring*, p. 28.

73. Pp. 158ab, 159a.

74. *Bucer*, p. 465.

75. *Tetrachordon*, p. 682. For contemporary interpretations of the Pauline analogy which deal primarily with the marriage of Christ and the Church rather than that of man and wife, see John Preston, *The Churches Marriage* (London, 1638), pp. 1–71; Francis Rous, *The Misticall Marriage Betweene Christ and His Church* (London, 1653), pp. 1–351; John Robinson, *An Ap-*

The special nature of the marriage bond was considered the
reason for its constant use in Scripture, where it is treated by
interpreters as a paradigm or metaphor for the relationship
of Christ and his Church:

> The cause wherefore the holy Ghost represents this love and
> union between these two ["Christ Jesus and his Spouse"],
> in all this Song [of Solomon], by the similitude of matri-
> moniall conjunction, is, because in all other bonds of love
> or friendship, there is not either so sacred a ground of so holy
> and particular intire affection, nor such a communion of so
> deere things, as hearts, bodies, and goods, nor so strait a con-
> junction of parties, becoming thereby one flesh, not so durable
> for time, being dissolvable only by death, and the effect
> divine rather than humane, God using men thereby but as in-
> struments to propagate his Church. Therefore the Holy Ghost
> being to represent unto us that which is otherwise in it selfe
> unconceivable, could chuse no fitter similitude then this
> affection and union matrimoniall: Therefore also it is, that
> in other places of Scripture the Church is called the Bride and
> the Lamb's wife. *Rev.* 21.9 and *Ioh.* 3.29. our Savior is called
> the bridegroom, & the Church his bride; whereby is evident,
> though this Bride and bridegroome bee not named by any
> proper names in all this Song, yet that it is without all con-
> troversie, that Christ and his Church are meant.[76]

The *Song of Solomon* not only taxed the exegetical powers of
tender-minded divines but provided a fund of images which

pendix to Mr. Perkins his Six Principles of Christian Religion (London,
1656), p. 5; Arthur Jackson, Annotations Upon the five Books immediately
following the Historical Part of the Old Testament (London, 1658), 2, 119;
Henry Vertue, Christ and the Church (London, 1659), pp. 241–54. The language of Rous' meditation most nearly resembles that of Milton in the divorce tracts, even though Rous is speaking of a figurative marriage and Milton of a literal one. See Rous, pp. 22–24, 27–28. He also anticipates the concept of the "Paradise within" occasionally: see sig. A2ᵛ–3ʳ and p. 310.

76. William Guild, Loves Entercovrs between The Lamb & his Bride,
Christ and his Church (London, 1658), pp. 1–2.

could be transferred to matters of mere earthly matrimony.
One such image was that of the garden. The garden appears in
the *Song of Solomon* as a metaphor for the delights which the
wife offers the husband. The opulence of the imagery suggested
to the interpreters of Scripture the perfect garden, Eden.
Eden then easily became associated, by virtue of the analogy which
was thought to control the entire work, with the Church itself.[77]

The seventeenth century defined the roles of husband and
wife unambiguously; if matrimonial conversation was unhappy,
the fault was not the lack of a fully articulated ideal. Briefly,
the wife was to obey, the husband to love. Samuel Hieron provides an adequate résumé of the duties proper to each: "[Desire
to know] what authoritie tempered with loue and cōpassion,
and freed from all bitternes, is cōmitted to the husband; what
obedience, & submission with reurence is commended to the
wife; what faithfulnes in matrimoniall duties either to other is
enioyned; what prouidence and care is expected of the man, &
what assistance and helpe of the woman."[78] Neither the husband's authority over his wife nor the reasons for it were
questioned. Man was the "king in his family" because woman
was "not altogether equall" to him, though her right to govern
in her own sphere was not doubted.[79] Man's superiority to
woman could be proved by various means; William Gouge's
argument runs through a cycle of the acknowledged facts that
God gave man authority, that nature made him taller, that the
Bible uses titles which imply precedence, that he is head to his
wife as Christ is head to his Church, that he was created first,
and that his clothing displays his greater dignity and strength.[80]

---

77. John Robotham, *An Exposition On the whole booke of Solomons
Song, Commonly called the Canticles* (London, 1651), pp. 498–503, 624;
Jackson, 2, 182; Guild, pp. 187–88, 190, 232–33, passim. Guild also uses terms
derived from matrimonial tracts and decrees—*amor benevolentiae and àmor
complacentiae*—as spiritual metaphors. *Amor benevolentiae* is associated
with God's election of the sinner to salvation, *amor complacentiae* with His
delight in His Elect (pp. 6, 59–60).

78. *Sermons,* p. 412.

79. Whately, *Bride-Bush,* p. 16.

80. Pp. 158ab, 159a.

William Ames argues that the husband is the proper ruler of the household because his knowledge is greater than that of his wife; Ames does not have to argue the latter cause. The man is better able to evaluate his wife's honor and equality as well as the implications of their quarrels; he knows more readily the duties of both; and he can foresee the consequences of their mutual acts.[81] Others argue that male virtue exceeds female, "*multis parasangis*"; that man's authority is implicit in the title "image of God"; that man has a "double priority" over woman simply by virtue of his male sex and his office of husband; and that man's appearance, stature, and titles taken together prove his superior worth—an argument Milton himself uses in his description of Adam in *Paradise Lost.*[82]

The controversy over the status and character of women which had darkened the career of the Wife of Bath was still alive in mid-seventeenth-century England. The period of the Civil War was not marked by any notable anti-feminist attacks, but there were a number of ephemeral and satiric remonstrances, petitions, and "parliaments of women," supposedly composed by the wives of the City, which represented women as lecherous, vain, stupid, lazy, and shrewish. These pamphlets are parodies of more serious complaints against the political decisions of the country's leaders, and their wit is limited to the "unconscious" double-entendre. The City wives mourn the absence of the Cavaliers who provided them with amusement and diversion. Political implications are minor; the wars are presented from the point of view of suppressed instinct rather than factionalism, the controversy over church government, the growing tyranny of the army, or any other official cause; and the mood of the pieces is often comic rather than critical. As anti-feminist documents—if they can be called that—they are written in a tone which almost neutralizes indignation or resentment. These petitions seem to have disappeared after the Licensing Act of

81. *Commentary on Peter,* in *Workes,* (London, 1643), pp. 66–67.
82. W. L. *The Incomparable Jewell,* p. 31 (virtue is not used here to refer to mere manliness and physical strength); Ussher, p. 104; Hardy, p. 21; Whately, *Bride-Bush,* p. 16.

1647, but they appear again in less than ten years. Although
no one could have taken them seriously, they indicate a tradition
of popular anti-feminism.

On the other hand, the spirit of Juvenal's invective against
women often entered the courtesy book, particularly in those sections dealing with the dangers of matrimony. John Osborn, the
Austin Feverel among courtesy writers, is only one example of
the misogynist who purports to write a book of advice. *Pray be
not Angry* by "G. Thorowgood" is for the most part a satire
upon women, although his intention, like that of other courtesy
writers using the same tactic, is to provide the innocent reader
with a safe substitute for firsthand experience.[83] Thorowgood
seeks to enlighten those who want to marry, but his praise of
good women seems offhand and dispirited by comparison with
his coarse but lively condemnations of bad women:

> When a woman wanteth any thing, she will flatter and speak
> fair; not much unlike the flattering Butcher, who gently
> claweth the Ox when he intendeth to knock him on the
> head. Nay more, they are called Night-Crows, for that com-
> monly in their Chamber they will make request for such
> toys, as cometh in their heads in the day. Women know the
> time to work their craft; for in the night they will work a man
> like Wax, and draw him like as the Adamant doth the Iron:
> and having once brought him to the bent of her Bow, then
> she makes request for a Gown of the new fashion stuff, for a
> Petticoat of the finest Stammel, or for a Hat of the newest
> fashion: and will never be quiet, if her mind be set upon a
> thing, till she have it. So that if her husband put her off with
> delays, then her forehead will butt full of frowns, as if she
> threatned to make Clubs Trump, and he (poor soul) never a
> black Card in's hand: For with her cruel tongue she will ring
> him such a peal, that one would think the Devil were come

83. London, 1656. The intention is one of which the *Areopagitica* ap-
proves; it is precisely the lack of experience with women, whether vicarious
or real, that Milton sees as the chief circumstance which can easily prevent
the holy man from making the right choice in marriage.

from hell, calling of him Rogue, Rascal, Wittal, Sot, &c. saying, she could live without such a faggot-fac'd hornified
Coxcomb, as he, with a wannion to him. . . .

Who would impoverish himself, to enrich such Harlots, to
make them swim in their silks, and make Gill a Gentlewoman,
insomuch that she careth not a peny for the finest, nor a fig for
the proudest: she is as good as the best, although she have
hardly as much honesty as will serve her own turn, suffering
every mans fingers as deep in the dish, as thine are in the
platter, and every man to angle where thou castest thy *hook,*
holding up to all that come, not much unlike a Barbers Chair,
that so soon as one Knave is out, another is in, a common
hackney for every one that will ride, a boat for every one
to row in.[84]

A more significant contribution to the literature of anti-
feminism during the period of Milton's divorce tracts is a strange
defense of wife-beating by Moses à Vauts, who claims to be an
immigrant Jewish convert to Christianity. Moses à Vauts rep-
resents an extreme position on the question of authority in the
household, and he reduces the wife to the status of a servant.
What he says of the reasons for the husband's precedence over
his wife is in large measure a restatement of the principles of
Gouge and other divines, principles which the idealizers of
women were to refute by the simple device of making counter-
claims.[85]

Many of the funeral sermons printed in the seventeenth
century were essentially eulogies of women; and some of them
attributed the virtues of one woman to her sex generally.[86]
But there were also works which attempted to present an argu-

84. Thorowgood, sig. A3ʳ-A3ᵛ.
85. Moses à Vauts, *Husband's Authority,* pp. 45, 46.
86. Benjamin Spencer, Ἀφωνόλογος. *A Dumb Speech* (London, 1646);
Edward Whatman, *Funeral Obseqvies to the Right Honourable the Lady
Elizabeth Hopton* (London, 1647); J. Longe, *An Epitaph on the late deceased,
that truely-Noble and Renowned Lady Elizabeth Cromwel* (London, 1655);
Shaw, *Mistris Shawes Tomb-stone;* Edward Reynolds, *Mary Magdalens Love
to Christ* (London, 1659).

ment for the superiority of all women. A rhymed translation of
Agrippa's *The Glory of Women* appeared in 1652;[87] John
Heydon published a defense of women in *Advice to a Daughter*
which was precipitated by Osborn's attack in the *Advice to
His Son;*[88] and in 1677 an argument for feminine equality by
Poulain de la Barre was translated into English.[89]

Agrippa's defense is a hyperbolic work which, with the least
touch of irony, might have been transformed into satire. Agrippa
goes so far as to exculpate Delilah, Medea, and Clytemnestra
by placing all the blame, contrary to tradition, upon their
husbands,[90] and to defend women's right to preach, which he
says is denied them by men out of jealousy:

> Men do forbid them publickly to preach
> The Word of God, as holy Scriptures teach;
> For it appears unto each vulgar eye,
> That Joel saith, Women shall Prophesie;
> So was it done in the Apostles time,
> The wife of Simeon with more did clime
> Up to the Pulpit, and instruct by rule,
> As well the solid wise man, as the foole:
> But now of late, so large mens sins are grown,
> That they usurp Gods wisdome as their own;
> They do the Women of their rights beguile,
> By breathing out invective speeches vile,
> Against their fame because they could not get
> Each man his soul in such a Cabinet.
>
> . . . . .
>
> 'Tis not by Rule, nor by divine Command,
> By which they take and hold the upper hand;
> Nor is't by title or possession right,
> But strength of arm, the Law that's called might.[91]

87. Trans. H. C. (London, 1652).
88. 2d ed. London, 1659.
89. François Poulain de la Barre, *The Woman as Good as the Man,* trans.
A.L. (London, 1677).
90. Agrippa, p. 27.
91. Ibid., pp. 44–45.

The revilers of females had declared the exact opposite of what
Agrippa was ready to assert—that woman is superior because of
her spirituality, her more dignified and noble name (denoting
"things inspired with lives"—the more favorable etymology of
Eve), and her preeminent beauty; because, unlike Adam, she
was created in Paradise; because she was created last (and is
therefore the creature in whom God sums up all that he had
created before); and because except for Adam's rib she was completely the handiwork of God, unlike Adam, who was formed
out of the slime of the earth.[92] Agrippa introduces other arguments whose sophistry is equal to these—or, for that matter,
to the anti-feminists' arguments. Agrippa's most flagrant distortion of what was regarded as incontrovertible truth by the
other side is contained in his discussion of responsibility for the
Fall:

> Man was charged by the Divine Decree,
> He should not touch the good and evill tree:
> 'Twas man alone to whom the charge was said,
> So 't must needs be so, for woman was not made:
> Therefore 'twas man, and man alone did sin,
> By reason that the charge was made to him:
> So then we drew (if Scripture we'l believe)
> Our former sins from Adam, not from Eve:
>
> .   .   .   .   .
>
> 'Twas not for eating, God did Eve accuse,
> But that she did not Sathan's tempts refuse;
> Not that the crime by woman was began,
> But as she gave occasion to the man:
> She first was snared in the Devils wile,
> And thus deceiv'd strove others to beguile:
> Poor Adam to his knowledge did transgresse,
> So did not Eve, which makes her sin the lesse:
> Satan cast woman with an envious fall,
> Because of creatures she's the best of all:
> Saint Bernard saith, the Devill did admire

92. Ibid , pp. 1–9.

To see her face, her beauty hatch'd a fire
In Satan's brest, which suddainly arose
Just like the burnings which the Bellows blows:
And whilst he stood, he did in envy swell.
Because that Eve in honour did excell.[93]

The virulence of John Heydon's response to Osborn's courtesy
book is dissipated largely in abusive epithets, yet a hysterical
tone emerges here and there in *Advice to a Daughter,* and the
unimaginative plan of the book—a series of counterstatements
refuting Osborn—does not lighten this impression.[94] However,
Heydon's statements about women often have a welcome rea-
sonableness when set beside the exaggerated claims of Agrippa,
the equally strained denunciations of the misogynists, or
Heydon's own abuse of Osborn. Heydon finds women superior
in virtue, but frail—capable of greater good and greater evil
than men. Women's subjection to man is the result of Eve's
sin, not of any natural inferiority.[95] But as a wife her chief
virtue is to respond to her husband's temperament and moods;
in Heydon, as in most religious writers, the wife's chief virtue
is her pliability:

nothing pleases her that doth not him, she is relative in all,
and he without her but half himself. . . . She frames her nature
unto his howsoever; the *Hyacinth* follows not the Sun more
willingly; stubbornness and obstinacy are herbs that grow
not in her Garden, she leaves talking to the Gossips of the
Town, and is more seen than heard.[96]

For all her subjection to man, woman's anatomical complexity
argues, for Heydon, her greater spiritual perfection. Furthermore, man is incomplete without woman, since our idea of
humanity includes both of them. There are curious Platonic
overtones in the assertion that Adam and Eve are therefore,

93. Ibid., pp. 17–19.
94. Heydon claimed to have written the book in sixteen days (sig. 4ᵛ).
95. Ibid., pp. 64, 59–60.
96. Ibid., p. 56.

in a way, one being, and that God's creation of man is concluded only in marriage: "when the husband and the wife are together, the world is contracted in a bed."[97] Although Heydon does not share Milton's "modern" view of likeness of disposition, or compatibility, as a necessity of true marriage, he does emphasize feminine equality in spiritual matters. He is, therefore, closer to a firm assertion of a special companionship as an ideal of marriage than most other contemporary writers.

> *a woman with a wise soul* is the fittest companion for man, otherwise God would have given him a friend rather than a Wife. A wise Wife comprehends both sexes; she is woman for her body, and she is man within, for her soul is like her Husbands. It is the Crown of blessings, when in one woman a man finds a Wife and a friend.[98]

Poulain de la Barre's *The Woman as Good as the Man* was translated and published in England in 1677, four years after its appearance in France. It is a book which could hardly have been written or approved of in England during the Interregnum; not only would its view of women have been unorthodox, but its use of the Bible is minimal, and its argumentation, unlike Agrippa's, is rational. For one thing, the work extols common sense, as though the Bible had no special authority in respect to woman's place in the universe. For another, it takes a detached view of precedents instead of employing received opinions, biblical sanctions, and familiar catch-phrases as solid proof. And finally, it unequivocally asserts feminine equality in all respects—even that of potential physical strength. Poulain states in his preface that he wishes to have the issue of feminine equality taken seriously and has therefore adopted a philosophical rather than a "gallant" style of discourse.[99] His view of women as victims of inferior education rather than as natural inferiors is complemented by a plea for equal education. In both purposes his work advances the

97. Ibid., pp. 60–61, 65.
98. Ibid., p. 69.
99. Poulain, pp. 148–49; sig. A5ᵛ.

"reasonable" idea of women which was to dominate later social attitudes.

Poulain's most formidable opponents, of course, are Scripture itself and the Fathers of the Church, both full of assertions which the anti-feminists could fall back upon for defense. Poulain unfalteringly argues against the notion that the Bible defines women as inferior creatures. Men cannot extrapolate "Nature" from the "Law" of the Bible without exquisite caution:

The *Scripture* speaketh not a word of Inequality: And, as the end of it is only to serve Men for a Rule in their Conduct, (according to the Notions which it gives of Justice); So, it leaves to every one the Liberty, to judge as well as he can of the natural (and true) state of Things. And, if we mind it, all the Objections which are drawn therefrom, are but Sophisms of Prejudice; whereby sometimes, *Men* understand (of all *Women*) Passages, which only agree to some few in Particular: Sometime they refer to Nature, that which only flowes from Education or Custom, and that which sacred Authors have spoken with Relation to their own Times.[100]

Poulain's social aim was to raise the standard of education for women. He not only attempts to prove that they are equal to men in common sense, natural eloquence, innate virtue, and ratiocinative power, but he also argues that typically feminine weaknesses—timorousness, credulity, superstition, tale-telling, curiosity, inconstancy, artifice, and malice—are in fact evidence of potential virtues that have been debased by false education into vices.[101] Swift was to use much the same argument in the satire against female education in Parts One and Four of *Gulliver's Travels,* and at times Poulain himself shares the darker vision of the satirist:

In all that which is taught to *Women,* do we see any thing that tends to solid instruction? It seems on the contrary, that

100. Ibid., sig. I 9ᵛ-10ʳ.
101. Ibid., pp. 163–76.

men have agreed on this sort of education, of purpose to abase their courage, darken their mind, and to fill it only with vanity, and fopperies; there to stifle all the seeds of Vertue, and Knowledge, to render useless all the dispositions which they might have to great things, and to take from them the desire of perfecting themselves.[102]

In fact, for Poulain the one advantage that men have over women is the superior privilege accorded them by civil law; so far as nature and natural right are concerned, the sexes are indistinguishable and inherently equal. Poulain proclaims woman man's superior in one respect, however, just as Milton and almost every other writer on the question of the differences between male and female do, and his tone here is playful: "if what thy can performe by the inside of the Head, renders them (at least) *Mens* Equals; the Out-side seldome ever failes, to render them absolutely their Mistresses."[103]

Poulain's attempt to clear the air of controversy was the culmination of a cultural process already under way even in England in the middle years of the seventeenth century. But unlike Poulain, divines and courtesy writers tended to rely on biblical or hermeneutic authority to present a view of women which, while not extenuating their role in the Fall of Man and other Old Testament catastrophes, set their virtues on at least an equal footing with their moral failures. In 1646, Thomas Moore the Elder was glossing the "silly women" of Paul's second epistle to Timothy, 3, to show that men and women are equal in divine grace and that the phrase was a term of opprobrium only by virtue of its application to men whose moral weakness was like the (in itself innocent) physical weakness of women.[104] William Hill, in 1660, was carefully dividing women into worldly, virtuous, and vicious types. In spite of the harshness of his preface, the text of Hill's *A New-Years-Gift for Women* is

102. Ibid., p. 162.
103. Ibid., p. 153.
104. Thomas Moore, *A Discovery of Seducers that creep into Houses* (London, 1646), p. 7.

filled with examples of good women.[105] There is no satire in the
work, and the author's claim that he loves and honors women
in spite of his own matrimonial experience (Hill was deserted
by his second wife) is well borne out by the evidence. He emphasizes women in the New Testament who were representatives
of love, sorrow, and the special grace of God.[106]

Possibly the anonymous *A Brief Anatomie of Women: Being
an Invective Against, and Apologie for, The Bad and Good of
That Sexe*[107] comes as close as anything, in its severely di-
chotomized point of view, to recording the tension felt during
the seventeenth century in trying to reconcile feminist and anti-
feminist positions. This pamphlet does not try to reconcile
them. It merely states mutually contradictory theses—that
women are detestable and that women are admirable—with
equal vigor. It is characteristic of the type to which this pamphlet belongs that the moment at which the argument is inverted is announced in religious terms; the implication throughout the work is that woman sums up the extremes of evil and
good:

> If we consider (how mans fall from that estate of grace and
> innocency wherein he was first placed, was acted and brought
> to passe by woman) we also find that the heavenly Creator
> (out of his infinite and unsearchable wisdom) so ordained that
> mans salvation proceded from woman also; so that by them
> came death, & by them likewise we were restored to life: what
> creature can be more excellent than that whom God hath
> made an instrument to act so great a work.[108]

The matrimonial writers understood St. Paul's dictum,
"Husbands, love your wives," in the light of the husband's
right of authority. Since the husband had superior power, love
was enjoined by St. Paul to temper the husband's exercise of it.

105. Pp. 1–2, 31–32.
106. Ibid., sig. A8ᵛ; pp. 31–32.
107. London, 1653.
108. Ibid., p. 4.

Love is the proper duty of the husband because men are "apt to be defective in this." By comparison with the writers' praise of conjugal love, this contradictory view seems remarkably unsentimental; love is a duty only in the sense of being a modification of a more essential obligation—to rule the wife. Love becomes a means of subjecting the woman, or of persuading her to submit herself to her husband.[109] The relationship between wisdom and love in the use of authority is fully set out by Dod and Cleaver and by Gouge.[110] Yet these writers did not deny that the love should be heartfelt, rather than merely one of the forms of behavior. Hardy declares that man ought to take contentment in enjoying his wife,[111] and Gouge not only calls affection necessary but roundly condemns stoicism in marriage.[112] In any case, a sincere affection for one's wife together with the consciousness of authority helps to maintain the proper domestic harmony.

The first epistle of St. Peter provided further support for this view of the matrimonial relationship; the chief offenses of the husband were in not loving his wife and in displaying a lack of wisdom toward her.[113] William Whately summarizes the husband's proper conduct most fully; he emphasizes the importance of wisdom, mildness, and justice. Wisdom ideally was a mark of the husband's commands, which should be sensible in themselves and should involve important issues. Mildness was a mark of the husband's reproofs, which should be made softly and discreetly. The husband was to remember that the wife was nearly equal to her husband, not a slave, and hence to be gently and "familiarly" treated. Skill and affection, not violence, were to be his means of rule. However, in important matters the husband had the unquestioned right to exert his authority per-

109. Hardy, pp. 6, 12. See also p. 5.
110. Dod and Cleaver, *Household Government*, sig. F8^r; Gouge, sig. A4^v-B1^r.
111. Hardy, p. 6.
112. Gouge, pp. 47b–48a, 209a–209b. See also Smith, pp. 30, 31–34.
113. Nicholas Byfield, *The Marrow of the Oracles of God* (11th ed. London, 1640), p. 65.

emptorily. Mildness was not to neutralize his primary right. Finally, justice was a mark of his exercise of power: he was obliged to maintain his wife, to refrain from commanding unlawful things, and to be sure that he was not reproving her mistakenly or harshly.[114] Other writers enlarge upon these basic assertions of duty. Ruling by wisdom involved, among other things, learning the wife's nature and yielding in strife over unimportant issues; if the man lacked wisdom, he lost the right to his wife's obedience.[115] Tenderness is encouraged by references to the wife's dependence, her equality as a human being, her honor as a wife, and the intimacy of her relationship with the husband. The biblical metaphor of the vine supported by the house became an image of feminine subjection and reliance upon the graver and stronger male. Hardy uses it to indicate that the woman is subject but not slave. He sees the creation of Eve from Adam's rib as evidence of the same truth, although the rib frequently exemplified the oneness of matrimony and the closeness of the matrimonial bond.[116] Bishop King sees the rib as a reminder that all quarrels between man and wife are like internal disorders.[117] In any case, authority was to be tempered "with equality"; the wife was "to bee gouerned with loue, not overruled by tyranny,"[118] and was obliged to be honored as her condition implied.[119] This meant that wife-beating was immoral and an offense against one's own flesh.[120] Any attempt to create fear or to compel, drive, or constrain the wife offended against the concept of mutually willed action which was the implied ideal of matrimony.[121]

114. *Bride-Bush*, pp. 22–26; 27–29; 32–34.

115. Smith, pp. 28–29.

116. Hardy, pp. 6, 7–8.

117. King, *Vitis Palatina*, p. 30. Both the rib and the vine become common metaphors for describing the relationship of married men and women, and their significance is discussed more fully later in this chapter.

118. Wilkinson, *The Merchant Royall*, p. F3ʳ.

119. King, pp. 27–28.

120. Smith, p. 34 (for the opposite point of view, see Moses à Vauts); Perkins, *Christian Oeconomie*, pp. 123–27.

121. Secker, *Wedding Ring*, pp. 39–40.

The other duties of the husband were normally related to
his position of dominance over his wife. All his virtuous acts
were also examples by which he could maintain his authority.
If he avoided bitterness, prodigality, and unchastity, he could
the more easily control these vices in his mate.[122] The virtues
enjoined upon the husband—patience, bounty, familiarity,
sobriety, prudence,[123] mindfulness of joy, and holiness[124]—
were, like his wisdom, love, and provision of physical necessities
for his wife,[125] reflections of a superior moral nature which was
to provide guidance and support for the weaker vessel. Above
all, the husband was to remember the wife's fragility: when the
gentleness of the husband is urged, the wife is often compared to
a precious piece of Venetian glass.[126]

The other injunction of St. Paul, "Wives, obey your husbands," provided the key to all instructions of the wife in her
duties. Feminine submissiveness was the natural complement
to masculine authority. In sum, the wife was to be "loving,
obedient, helpfull."[127] But such advice really implies a double
role for the wife. She was not merely to obey passively; in helping her husband she was performing services which were also
demonstrations of her role and her particularly feminine
capabilities.

Yet the passive virtues receive the most attention among the
matrimonial writers, perhaps because women subjected themselves to men only with some difficulty. The matrimonial writers
attempted to achieve through instruction what the husband
tried to achieve through love. For them, the acknowledgement
of inferiority was the source of wifely virtue. They praise only
the behavior proper to that acknowledgment, since "out of
place, out of peace." Obedience in all lawful things is the only

122. Whately, *Bride-Bush*, p. 20.
123. Crompton, *Wedding-Ring*, p. 33.
124. W.L., *The Incomparable Jewell*, pp. 40–41.
125. Smith, p. 31; King, pp. 23, 24.
126. Abbott, *Christian Family*, p. 45; Edmund Reyner, *Precepts for Christian Practice* (London, 1645), p. 160.
127. Crompton, p. 31.

way to achieve tranquillity in marriage, and the wife's reverence toward her husband should be essentially that of a servant, though tempered by "love" and "familiarity."[128] In a remarkable little sermon which is essentially a full-dress Elizabethan conceit based on the biblical comparison of a wife to a merchant ship, Robert Wilkinson defines the virtues of the wife, practically all of which share the qualities of retirement and dependence.[129] Vives identifies the wife's special duty as "peacefulness,"[130] and the qualities of reverence, obedience, modesty, retirement, silence, patience, and compliance characterize ideal wifely behavior for most other matrimonial writers.[131]

The woman's gravest offense against her office as wife was the sin of ambition, the attempt to set herself above her husband's rightful authority. It manifested itself in various ways: in prideful behavior, in unwillingness to subject herself, in nagging and quarreling, and in general troublemaking.[132] Wilkinson likens the quarreling wife to a man-of-war and the usurping wife to a pirate ship.[133] The only way of overcoming this sin was through subjection, the proper disposition of the wife. Ames defines "subjection" as conjugall feare" (that sort of reverence due a husband), "chastity of conversation," and "meeknesse and mildnesse."[134] Gouge also defines it clearly and completely as various duties: "The wife must recognize the husband's superiority; fear him; show him reverence & obedience; depend upon his consent and his will in household matters; accept his criticism; be content with her husband's possession and income, subject herself to him lawfully and cheerfully."[135] Subjection did not mean only that the wife was to

128. Whately, *Bride-Bush*, pp. 36, 42, 37.
129. Sig. C2^v-D3^r.
130. Vives, *Christen Woman*, sig. Yiii^{r-v}.
131. See Dod and Cleaver, *Household Government*, sig. O3^v, F3^r; Smith, pp. 35–38; Jeremy Taylor, *Works*, pp. 272–79.
132. Perkins, *Christian Oeconomie*, pp. 129–33.
133. Sig. D3^r.
134. *Commentary on Peter*, in *Workes*, p. 66.
135. Sig. A4^v.

yield to her husband in matters morally indifferent, or that she was simply to show him reverence in her gestures, speech, and actions.[136] She was also obliged to *love* her husband by "fearing" him; that is, by having no impulse to rebel. She was to show him "such an affection as yieldeth chearfull subjection." As man was bound to love, his wife was bound to fear.[137]

However, the wife's more active virtues, as outlined by the matrimonial writers, imply a far handsomer view of feminine spirit and strength. "Man is stronger by his wife," says Henry Smith. Man is frail and needs the help of his wife, her physical and spiritual aid: "she is called a *Helper* to helpe him in his business, to help him in his labours, to helpe him in his troubles, to helpe him in his sicknes, like a woman-physician; sometime with her strength, and sometime with her counsell." The names given to the wife imply an active role: goodwife, yokefellow, helper, comforter, housewife.[138] The household virtues share with those of submission the highest praise; Crompton names industry, vigilance, providence (in the ordering of domestic affairs), wisdom, and discretion, along with fidelity and piety, as proper to the woman.[139] Her sobriety and godly devotion were supremely necessary to domestic order.[140] And her wastefulness and idleness, as well as her rebelliousness and forwardness, are given biblical condemnation, should she be guilty of them.[141] Finally, her example has its own efficacy; if her husband is vicious the fault may well be hers.[142]

The commonplace reference to woman as the rib of Adam usually implied some view of the use of authority in marriage. The fact that Eve was created from a rib rather than from some part of the head or the foot supplied a precise analogy to the wife's position of subjection but not servitude to her husband.

136. Ibid., p. 196[a–b]; Hardy, p. 22.
137. Hardy, p. 19.
138. Smith, pp. 9, 34–35.
139. Crompton, pp. 3–4.
140. Wilkinson, sig. E2[v], E4[r].
141. Byfield, *Marrow*, pp. 64–65.
142. Crompton, p. 34.

And the nearness of the rib to the heart implied the affection which man was to feel for his mate. The husband's kind of authority and the love with which he should temper it are summed up in the metaphor. But the reference could be turned toward either the wife or the husand to remind them of particular duties. To Parsons it is a reminder of the inseparability of marriage, and therefore of fidelity; to Ussher it is symbolic of the subjection of woman and the nearness of man and wife; to Hardy it denotes the "fellow-ship" of the wife with her husband,[143] but to Bullinger it provides a reason for the helpfulness of the wife: "Yet was she not made of the head: for the husband is the head & Maister of the wyfe. Neither was she made of the feete (as though thou mightest spurn her away from thee, and nothing regard her) but even out of thy side, as one that is set next unto man, to be his helpe and companion."[144]

Woman as Adam's rib suggested to Secker the protection (and the mildness) due the wife: "as the use of the arme is to keep off blowes from the body, so the office of the husband is to ward off blowes from the wife."[145] The rib was not an entirely stable symbol; it could be made to express the materiality of feminine nature, woman's lack of value and dignity, or her sinfulness (the rib being crooked); and it could be used to refer to something as antithetical to these as the intimacy and love which typify the marriage bond.[146] In other words, the rib could symbolize matrimonial equality, male authority, feminine inferiority, or mutual affection, depending upon the bias of the interpreter or the particular point he wished to emphasize rhetorically. All of these concepts play a significant part in Milton's treatment of the image.

Another metaphor, of classical as well as biblical origins, that of the vine, was helpful in designating the reliance of the wife

143. Parsons, p. 21; Ussher, p. 107; Hardy, pp. 7–8.
144. Bullinger, *Christian Matrimony*, fol. 2ᵛ.
145. Secker, p. 40.
146. *A Briefe Anatomie of Women*, p. 1; Moses à Vauts, p. 68; Needler, *Expository Notes*, pp. 54–55.

upon the husband. The wife, supported by the husband as the vine by the house, depended on that support for her fruitfulness and her strength. But the image of the vine could also specify the expectations which the husband might have of his wife, and it therefore became the symbol of feminine virtues, characteristics, weaknesses, and matrimonial assistance. It became, in short, more than an emblem of the matrimonial relationship, a symbol of woman herself. For Bishop King, the vine summed up the woman's tractability, sensitivity, and purity; the refreshment and comfort she offered to man; and her frailty.[147]

Milton uses both concepts of feminine virtue—the passive virtues of compliance and the active virtues of helpfulness—in his argument for divorce. As the previous chapter indicated, Milton was able to use the requisite of docility as a factor in the difficulty of choice; the easily led woman may be merely concealing the faults of sluggishness and torpor under the appearance of tractability; a man frequently could not know this until he had married. Yet the equal-but-inferior position accorded to women in the handbooks of matrimony works into Milton's argument in another way. Woman was made for marriage, whereas marriage was made for man.[148] Man is not limited by the same purpose as woman; the institution was created to serve his needs, whereas woman is the means by which his needs are served. Hence, for Milton divorce is not intended for wives in quite the same way as it is intended for husbands, simply because their relationship to the institution is different.[149] There are, certainly, causes for which the wife may divorce the husband; Milton seems to agree that the causes (including wife-beating) for which divorces were allowed to

147. Pp. 17–18. The analogy was also used profanely in *The Card of Courtship: or, the Language of Love* (London, 1653) to describe amorous embraces (p. 108). For a discussion of the tradition of the elm and vine as an emblem of marriage from Catullus through Heinrich Kleist, see Peter Demetz, "The Elm and the Vine: Notes Toward the History of a Marriage Topos," *PMLA, 73* (1958), 521–32.

148. *Tetrachordon*, p. 627.

149. *D and D*, p. 234.

women under the law of the Roman Empire, as listed by Bucer, are just.[150] Most divines argue that a wife can divorce a man for beating her (though of course only *a mensa et thoro*), since he violates her rights as a free-born person,[151] and Milton would have agreed that physical cruelty was a cause for divorce. But there is no suggestion in Milton's tracts that a wife may divorce her husband for not supplying her with the needs of her nature, for not fulfilling the ideal of matrimonial conversation, or for not being a "meet help." Her position simply does not give her the right to plead these causes. Submission to man is guaranteed by the Bible; the words which grant authority to man are the words of the "Spirit of God"—a very strong phrase: "If the Spirit of God wrote such aggravations as these, and as may be guest by these similitudes, counsels the man rather to divorce then to live with such a collegue, and yet on the other side expresses nothing of the wives suffering with a bad husband; is it not most likely that God in his Law had more pitty towards man thus wedlockt, then towards the woman that was created for another."[152] This authority gives man alone the right of divorcing a displeasing partner. Finally, obedience is to Milton, as it was to the other matrimonial writers, the essential posture of womanhood and ambition is its disfigurement. The fornication, or pollution, for which the Bible allowed divorce is, according to Milton, simply the disobedience, alienation of mind, or will-worship of the woman, since only this sin can violate the ordained hierarchy of marriage[153] Physical pollution merely disunites bodies, but the disunity created by a new "will" and center of authority in marriage corrupts the marriage itself.

But even though Milton shapes his argument to the conven-

150. *Bucer,* pp. 462–63.
151. Hardy, p. 16. But the Anglican Henry Hammond denies divorce to a woman for any reason—including the infidelity of the husband. He asserts that divorce is nowhere in the Old or New Testaments granted to women, and that family integrity is not so threatened by the husband's adultery as it is by the wife's *(A Practical Catechisme,* p. 80).
152. *D and D,* p. 324.
153. *Tetrachordon,* pp. 672–73.

tional aspects of feminine inferiority, he places far greater emphasis throughout the tracts on the active virtues of the woman. These he considers the chief value of womanhood. The essential nature of the wife is that she be a "help." God created woman for this aim alone, the "maine ends of marriage" being "helpe & solace."[154] God did not intend woman to be a "perpetuall torment" rather than a "meet help."[155] Therefore, if a wife cannot be a "help" meet for a man, he has made no marriage, and the divorce is, per se, already effected.[156]

The duties common to both husband and wife received less attention from the writers of matrimonial handbooks than the particular duties of each mate. Whately's *Bride-Bush*, however, sums up common obligations by distinguishing duties toward the mate from common duties toward the family.[157] Faithfulness was the primary virtue; William Gouge calls it the chief duty of marriage.[158] Common "helpfulness," another virtue, consisted of mutual aid in piety, health, and reputation: the partners were to pursue virtue in common, to help avoid or cure sickness, and to conceal each other's personal faults. Finally, they were to govern and maintain the family properly. Maintenance required the virtues of industry, frugality, and foresight; and government required piety, watchfulness, and harmony in approving or chastising offending children or servants. To these virtues might be added the politeness which Dod and Cleaver advise—the use of titles.[159] For titles demonstrate that sense of dignity and hierarchy which all the matrimonial writers praised as the mark of a well-ordered household life.

Exhortations to mutual piety as a proper means of governing a household impinged upon other aspects of matrimony such as the awareness of special virtue in choosing a marriage

154. Ibid., p. 691.
155. *Bucer*, p. 470.
156. *D and D*, p. 309.
157. Pp. 11–18.
158. P. 214.
159. *Household Government*, sig. N8ᵛ.

partner or the view of matrimony as an especially holy state.
Samuel Hieron advises choosing a mate who will lead one to
heaven, a mate not merely virtuous but zealous to inspire
virtue.[160] The wife was to be a "spiritual instructor" as well
as "servant" and "friend." The result of so much domestic piety
was to be an earthly marriage which prefigured the eternal marriage of the soul in heaven with the Lamb.[161]

Marriage had, of course, always been highly praised by
Protestant reformers, who regarded the institution of clerical
celibacy by the Roman church as a diabolical perversion of
Christian teaching. Calvin considered marriage a type of virginity and declared that what was necessary in some cases was
honorable in all.[162] English Protestants, high and low, never
tired of reiterating Calvin's position. The honor of marriage
in being the oldest calling of man[163] was coupled with a condemnation of the vow of single life as "a snare of conscience, and
the bond of impurity."[164]

Yet marriage is always acknowledged to have been more perfect before the Fall of Man, and the state of virginity acquired
what virtue it had only as a result of the Fall.[165] Milton uses
this common assumption of the debasement of marriage as an
argument in favor of Mosaic law, which allowed divorce and
therefore eased the difficulties confronted in marriage as a result of the Fall. Mosaic law helped fallen man to attain the
peace and contentment possible in marriage.[166] Indeed, for
Milton, marriage seems to be a corrective to the Fall, a condition
in which it is possible for man to recover some of the happiness
and freshness of the primitive world. Certainly man seeks in
marriage a kind of emotional fulfillment impossible in any other
condition. For this reason Milton upholds divorce as necessary;

160. Hieron, *A Helpe vnto Deuotion*, p. 407.
161. Wilkinson, sig. C2^r, C2^v.
162. *Institutes*, 2, 1254; *1*, 406; 2, 1257.
163. Smith, p. 10; see also Parsons, pp. 17 ff.
164. Ames, *Marrow*, p. 324.
165. Gouge, pp. 124^a–124^b.
166. *D and D*, pp. 308–20.

without it, an unhappy marriage will produce moral and religious infidelity—adultery or despair. In isolation, this position
seems uncompromisingly individualistic. But when taken in the
context of the marriage writers, it begins to reveal common
characteristics. Marriage conceived as a remedy for lust bears
interesting resemblances to Milton's conception of marriage,
not only as a remedy for a spiritual "burning." The matrimonial
writers were willing to assert that if a particular man stood
in need of marriage as a remedy, God would hear his request
for a meet wife.[167] The implication that some marriages are
divinely "arranged" seems to concede far more importance to
individual men than Milton's notion that God ordains only the
marriage of those suitable for one another and that He allows
civil divorce to those who are "unmeet."

Praise of the married state is so frequent among matrimonial
writers that William Whately's elaborate account of its disagree-
able possibilities is almost refreshing, in spite of its occasional
cynical tone.[168] But Whately's purpose is quite unlike Milton's.
Whately seeks to encourage caution or tolerance in marriage;
Milton argues for the rejection of intolerable conditions. Although Milton's argument explores the domestic and social as
well as personal ramifications of an unhappy marriage, his account of the moral disintegration of the unhappily married man
diminishes even Whately's lurid catalogue of evils.

Milton's myth—and his argument is almost that—is an inversion of the spiritual ascent of the platonic lover. Through
sensuous experience of love, followed by the absence of the be-
loved either through disdain or circumstance, the platonic lover
ascends to a notion of ideal love which enables him to reject
the less worthy delights of the flesh, whether or not these are
ever offered again. Milton's unfortunate *mari* undergoes a parallel descent through a similarly painful trial. His experience

167. John Dod and Richard Cleaver, *A Plaine and Familiar Exposition of
the Ten Commandements* (London, 1609), p. 287.
168. See *Bride-Bush*, pp. 40–68, especially pp. 40, 63, 65; and *Care-Cloth*,
p. 76.

of love in marriage is never fulfilled because though his body
is satisfied, his soul is parched; spiritual incompatibility lessens
even the fleshly satisfactions of matrimony. Furthermore, the
wife's constant presence produces a spiritual unrest inimical to
contemplative religious activity. This lack of serenity drives
the soul away from God. The husband not only cannot pray; he
falls to blaming God for his condition. He is reduced to the
level of bestial intercourse with an object for whom he feels no
human affection. Unlike the platonic lover who passes through
Eros to *Agape*, the mismatched husband passes through *Eros* to
Ate. If the object is unsuitable the sensuous experience which
can produce spiritual insight can also kill the spirit in a furious
kind of revenge.

Milton is in fact making use of the divines' view of marriage
as an aid to piety, a way to heaven, by presenting the ill effects of
an unhappy marriage in religious terms. He merely inverts the
position of the religious writers. If an ideal marriage properly
increases religious devotion, an unhappy marriage can lead to
blasphemy. Milton's argument has a number of applications:
(1) The man of melancholy temperament will be inclined to
feel the pain of the reprobate if his marriage is unhappy.[169]
(2) The discord of the matrimonial conversation can cause
despair when the unhappy man had prayed for a happy marriage:

> if he be such as hath spent his youth unblamably, and layd up
> his chiefest earthly comforts in the enjoyment of a contented
> mariage, nor did neglect that furderance which was to be ob-
> tain'd herein by constant prayers, when he shall find himselfe
> bound fast to an uncomplying discord of nature, or, as it oft
> happens, to an image of earth and fleam, with whom he lookt
> to be the copartner of a sweet and gladsome society, and sees
> withall that his bondage is now inevitable, though he be
> almost the strongest Christian, he will be ready to dispair in
> vertue, and mutin against divine providence: and this doubt-

169. *D and D*, pp. 354, 247.

les is the reason of those lapses and that melancholy despair which we see in many wedded persons, though they understand it not.[170]

(3) The tears of an unhappy husband will defile the altar of God. (4) The unmeet mate is as bad as an idolatress in forcing her husband's faith to dissolve.[171] The whole argument rests upon the belief that God is just. In not providing unhappy marriages with the cure of divorce, sanctioned by Old Testament law (unchanged by the Gospel), the commonwealth is guilty of undermining belief in divine justice. For if marriage is indivisible—the premise of the current divorce laws—then unhappy marriage is either the sign of God's displeasure or a perverse divine answer to a prayer for a "help meet." If the unhappy mate feels that he is worthy, then there is a contradiction between his estimate of himself and God's estimate of him. One of two consequences will follow: either despair over his spiritual condition or loss of faith.

Hypocrisy is another moral ill which may follow an unhappy marriage. Milton considers the falseness which ensues when love disappears and a marriage is "burst like a rotten thread" only one of the many sins which attend this condition,[172] but it is especially detestable to God because it violates the nature of marriage, which requires love.[173] On the other hand, to those who see a chance for merit in the difficulties of married life Milton argues that to do heroic good should not be forced by civil law and cannot be demanded by God. He drives home this position with a series of aphorisms which emphasize the necessity of human freedom in the exercise of virtue—a position similar to that of *Areopagitica:* "God loves not to plow out the heart of our endeavours with overhard and sad tasks. God delights not to make a drudge of vertue, whose actions must be all elective and unconstrain'd Forc't vertu is as a bolt overshot,

170. Ibid., p. 254.
171. Ibid., pp. 259, 260.
172. *Tetrachordon*, pp. 630–31.
173. *D and D*, p. 256; *Bucer*, p. 455.

it goes neither forward nor backward, & does no good as it
stands."[174]

Throughout his argument, Milton is in effect redefining God's
law as understood by his audience. He agrees with Bucer that
God is benevolent whereas the church is tyrannical.[175] Christ
did not alter the laws of marriage; the Gospel does not forbid
divorce.[176] Milton argues the latter point in two ways: in
Tetrachordon he says that Christ, in allowing divorce for no
cause but adultery, was speaking only to the Pharisees, whose
duplicity and distortion of the law was such that it had to be
counterbalanced by a statement recalling them to the original
state of virtue, heroic virtue now the gift only of those having
special grace (p. 668). Christ's statement is a deliberate ex-
aggeration, meant for the Pharisees, not for all Christians. In the
Doctrine and Discipline of Divorce Milton had used another interpretation: the statement was intended generally, but fornication was to be understood not as adultery but as any behavior
displeasing to the husband and engendering a rational suspicion
of adultery (p. 337).

Not only did Milton oppose the other matrimonial writers
on the significance of a bad marriage for personal virtue, but he
also argued the cause of social utility as upholding divorce, not
denying it. (Milton's argument must, however, be distinguished
from his definition of marriage which ignored larger social
implications.) The effects of an unhappy marriage upon the
person affect the family, state, and church. Continuation of such
a marriage diminishes man's secular and religious activity—
clearly not God's intention in creating marriage. Such a marriage is useless. The children of these marriages are the "children
of wrath"—in effect illegitimate and unregenerate. The loneliness which is increased with the burden of an unmeet mate is
dangerous both to the man and to the Commonwealth, and
moral order can be restored only through the reinstitution of

174. *D and D*, p. 342. See also p. 260.
175. *Bucer*, p. 431.
176. *D and D*, p. 329.

divorce. Milton catalogs the ill effects of continued matrimonial unhappiness in the *Doctrine and Discipline of Divorce*
(pp. 245–75) and in *Tetrachordon* (pp. 675–76).
The argument of Milton's divorce tracts is plainly founded
on the dualities of soul and body, essence and accident, "spirit"
and "letter." These dualities need not suggest any kind of ir-
reparable dichotomy; they are not evidence of a dissociation
of sensibility but of a logical and hierarchical distinction which
Milton finds useful in pleading his case. The precedence of
spirit over matter, of meaning over formal rule, of conscience
over statute, and of reason over apparent word—even scriptural
word—rather than any radical discontinuity between them,
furnishes Milton with his liveliest persuasive machinery. The
divines were willing to grant that discord was a function of contrary humors,[177] that love should be spiritual as well as physical,[178] that man and woman were to "dwell together in
coniugall vnity, hauing one heart and one soule,"[179] but not
that the failure of the spiritual bond should end the marriage.
For Milton, the institution of marriage when both parties are
unhappy is a Baconian idol, for "the ends why matrimony was
ordain'd, are certainly and by all Logic above the Ordinance it
self."[180]

177. Dod and Cleaver, *Household Government,* sig. N6ʳ–N8ᵛ.
178. Gouge, p. 209b.
179. Parsons, sig. A3ᵛ.
180. *Tetrachordon,* p. 628.

4

Ideal Marriage:

Paradise Lost

... that first mariage was our funerall:
One woman at one blow, then kill'd vs all,
And singly, one by one, they kill vs now.

John Donne, *Anniversaries,* I

Milton's concept of marriage was possible only to a man who saw the universe as a vast system of affinities and oppositions controlled by the grand principle of harmony. The Fall of Man had disrupted this element of hierarchy and synthesis; it had made the achievement of harmony in most cases a *difficulté vaincue* rather than a natural concomitant of man's being, birth, or station. Man was divided within himself, from his fellowman, and from God by the accidental discords of fallen nature which he could repair only through a rectification of his will and a restoration within his domestic, civil, and religious life of the decorum subverted by the Fall. Proof that the decorum persisted in spite of man's failure of attunement—that, indeed, the momentary disharmony merely enriched the harmonies that were in existence—was given to man in the Law and in the Redemption which freed man from the Law. And man's imperfect sense of the implications of divine revelation had been the source of both Milton's indignation and his sense of mission as a pamphleteer.

The relationship between the divorce tracts and *Paradise Lost* is manifold, since the marriage presented in the poem has moral, dramatic, and symbolic value. First of all, the poem can be read as the history of a marriage; Milton traces the relationship between Adam and Eve from God's creation of a help meet for Adam through the pure conversation of their married life to the point of rupture induced by disobedience, the mutual torment of their fallen marriage, and the reconciliation made possible through divine grace and Eve's proofs of her inescapable "fitness" for Adam. If she has been the instrument of his Fall, she is also the "help" of his fallen state. (God's institution of matrimony foresaw the full implication of the term "help meet for him.") The history of their marriage also dramatizes the condition of their souls. They respond to each other in accordance with their attunement to universal law. Their "conversation" thus becomes a series of tableaux which isolate the stages of the major action and concentrate its effects. Finally, the marriage of Adam and Eve as a symbol of appropriate conjunction is thematically echoed, varied, or distorted in the sexuality of angelic attraction and concord, the violent incestuous rape of Sin by Satan, the magnetism of the elements, and the mésalliance of sons of God and daughters of Cain. It would be possible to consider each of these uses of the marriage ideal separately, but since to a large extent their literary effectiveness in *Paradise Lost* depends upon their respective positions in the text, it seems wiser to follow Milton's order, which establishes a dialectic of its own.

It is not entirely accidental that the first figure in *Paradise Lost* to have female characteristics is Sin. She is not, of course, a woman, but an allegorical character, "double-form'd," who

> seem'd Woman to the waist, and fair,
> But ended foul in many a scaly fold
> Voluminous and vast, a Serpent arm'd
> With mortal sting.

> (II.650–53)

The unnaturally divided shape, both "Woman" and "Serpent," "fair" and "foul," emphasizes the discord between the appearance and reality of sin, its combined attractiveness and danger.

But unlike her obvious literary prototypes, Spenser's Error in
Book I of *The Faerie Queene* and the Harlot of the *Book of
Revelation,* Milton's Sin has a pronounced dramatic relevance.
She foreshadows the special relationship, founded on biblical
texts, which will exist between the Woman and the Serpent:
only Eve will be beguiled by Satan in the disguise of a Serpent;
and to woman will be given the honor of crushing the Serpent's
head beneath her heel. Furthermore, Sin foreshadows the seduction of Adam by Eve's attractiveness and by the deceptive concealment of her less honorable purposes. Sin epitomizes the
worst possibilities of ensnarement in womanhood, as she contrasts with the purity which will ultimately conquer her.

The relationship between Satan, Sin, and Death is a deliberate parody of both the Trinity and human domestic relationships. Sin is the image of Satan (II.756, 764), as the Son is the
image of the Father; Sin and Satan beget Death, the principle
of destruction, as the Father and Son generate the Holy Spirit,
the creative principle. As the Father, Son, and Holy Spirit share
mutual knowledge and love, mutual enmity at first characterizes
the relationship of Death and Satan, and Satan finds the images
he has forgotten, the images of himself, unrecognizable and
abominable:

> I know thee not, nor ever saw till now
> Sight more detestable than him and thee.
>
> (II.744–45)

The generation of Sin and Death is represented as a perversion
of human sexual relationships—the farthest pole from God's
self-love. Sin, "a Goddess arm'd," springs out of the head of
Satan, as Eve was created of Adam's rib to be his help. Satan's
love for his daughter combines incest with narcissism as Sin
describes it:

> I pleas'd, and with attractive graces won
> The most averse, thee chiefly, who full oft
> Thyself in me thy perfect image viewing
> Becam'st enamor'd.
>
> (II.762–65)

This incest is compounded by the maternal rape of Death, their Son, who begets upon his mother the hellhounds who try to consume her—symbols of the self-generated punishments of sin. This elaborate allegory even contains a declaration by Sin to Satan which, in its emphasis upon fidelity, obedience, and physical origin, might, except for its attribution of fatherhood, have been spoken by Eve to Adam:

> Thou art my Father, thou my Author, thou
> My being gav'st me; whom should I obey
> But thee, whom follow?
>
> (II. 64–66)[1]

Satan is reconciled with Sin and Death, and through them he gains access to the upper world. But their repulsiveness and their mutual detestation remain as reverse images of what Satan will find in Paradise.

Milton chooses Satan's consciousness as the instrument through which the reader first glimpses "Heaven on Earth" (IV.208). There are a number of reasons for this "point of view": it emphasizes the attractive beauty of Eden and of Adam and Eve, since even Satan recognizes his rudimentary, unfulfilled temptation to delight and pity in beholding them (IV.362–65; 372–75); it emphasizes the transiency of the state of innocence since we see it through the very threat to its existence, the power of negation; finally, it throws into high relief the damnation of Satan, who "saw undelighted all delight" (IV.286), was unable now to share a life of harmonious admiration and praise, and deeply envied Adam and Eve their state of wedded happiness. The sight of Adam and Eve in Paradise merely intensifies Satan's desire for revenge.

Two special aspects of the Garden itself are reflected in the matrimonial relationship of Adam and Eve before the Fall: its delightfulness as a place of pleasure, and the order which all things in it observe. The rich sensuousness of Milton's de-

---

1. Cf. *"Adam,* from whose dear side I boast me sprung,/ And gladly of our Union hear thee speak,/ One Heart, one Soul in both" (IX.965–67).

scription of the Garden is underscored by his continual use of
the epithet "delicious" and the words "bliss," "joy," and "delight."2 But Adam, Eve, and Satan all remark upon the fact
that the relationship between Adam and Eve, the enjoyment
of human love, is the epitome of all the delights of the Garden
itself. Adam with his first words addresses Eve as "Sole partner
and sole part of all these joys,/ Dearer thyself than all" (IV.411–
12), and Satan, consumed by lust and driven to frenzy by the
sight of their kisses, exclaims:

> Sight hateful, sight tormenting! thus these two
> Imparadis't in one another's arms
> The happier *Eden,* shall enjoy thir fill
> Of bliss on bliss, while I to Hell am thrust,
> Where neither joy nor love, but fierce desire,
> Among our other torments not the least,
> Still unfulfill'd with pain of longing pines.
>
> (IV.505–11)

Eve, in a long passage whose sophisticated repetition resembles
the chiming speeches of characters in Shakespeare's comedies—
for instance Orlando and the Duke Senior in *As You Like It,*
II.7.113–126—declares that none of the sensuous delights of
Paradise, pleasant as they are, is sweet to her without Adam's
presence (IV.641–56). Finally, both Adam and Eve, in the psalm
they sing to God before "thir shady Lodge," speak of "mutual
love, the Crown of all our bliss/ Ordain'd by thee." The relationship between Adam and Eve is fully chaste because it is
"wedded Love," human love informed by reason and by the
law of God, and also fully sexual:

> into thir inmost bower
> Handed they went; and eas'd the putting off
> These troublesome disguises which wee wear,
> Straight side by side were laid, nor turn'd I ween
> *Adam* from his fair Spouse, nor *Eve* the Rites
> Mysterious of connubial Love refus'd.
>
> (IV.738–43)

2. See IV.132, 251, 367, 369, 435, 508, 729, etc.

Milton's awareness of hierarchical order further determines the way in which he presents life in Eden. The physical appearance of the Garden itself is ordered; it is surrounded by a forest and thicket, topped by a wall over which trees appear, the highest tree in the Garden being the Tree of Life. And the first description of Adam and Eve suggests hierarchical differences, not only between man and animal but between man and woman; our first view of them is, in fact, as an emblem of perfect matrimony:

> both
> Not equal, as thir sex not equal seem'd;
> For contemplation hee and valor form'd,
> For softness shee and sweet attractive Grace,
> Hee for God only, shee for God in him:
> His fair large Front and Eye sublime declar'd
> Absolute rule; and Hyacinthine Locks
> Round from his parted forelock manly hung
> Clust'ring, but not beneath his shoulders broad:
> Shee as a veil down to the slender waist
> Her unadorned golden tresses wore
> Dishevell'd, but in wanton ringlets wav'd
> As the Vine curls her tendrils, which impli'd
> Subjection, but requir'd with gentle sway,
> And by her yielded, by him best receiv'd,
> Yielded with coy submission, modest pride,
> And sweet reluctant amorous delay.
>
> (IV.295–311)

This passage combines many of the traditional assertions about the male and female roles in marriage with Milton's own distinctive emphases. The contrasts between "contemplation" and "Grace," "valor" and "softness," seem particularly Miltonic. Intellect and courage, beauty and compliance, had pronounced masculine and feminine values for Milton. Man's superior understanding and strength gave him a natural authority over woman, just as the possession of "Truth, Wisdom, Sanctitude" by both Adam and Eve, in whom "The image of thir glorious

Maker shone," made them "Lords of all" (IV.290–94). Like the matrimonial handbooks, Milton argues the inequality of the sexes from the differences in their appearance; their hair, forehead, and eyes give evidence of different intellectual and moral powers. Adam's face expresses greater intelligence, curiosity, and heaven-directed vision; these give him "absolute rule" over Eve as well as the animals. Another traditional motif is the association of the "female" vine with dependence and submission on the one hand, and with frailty requiring gentleness of treatment on the other; it sums up the masculine obligation of authority exercised with mildness and love, and the feminine virtue of obedience. Other details enforce these contrasts: Adam's "shoulders broad," Eve's "slender waist," and the length, color, and arrangement of their hair. Eve's longer hair is a sign of her femininity; its veillike quality suggests her modesty and submission; it is unadorned because she exists in the state of natural innocence; its golden color suggests her greater physical beauty; its "wanton" curls suggest profusion, charming disorder, and the need for masculine government and authority. Finally, the paradoxes with which the passage ends help to characterize the mixture of retirement, love, modesty, sense of equality, and sense of shame which the matrimonial writers attributed to the ideal wife. The final line is particularly rich in possibilities of interpretation; not only is "amorous delay" paradoxical, implying desire and refusal, but "reluctant" can apply to either of the terms which follow it, or both together: *reluctant-amorous* (implying the conflict between modest unwillingness and passionate assent); *reluctant-delay* (implying the unwillingness to withhold submission, along with its necessity); *reluctant-amorous-delay)* (implying the unwillingness to show either indecent haste or misinterpreted indifference). "Sweet" has a similar complexity, since both the person and the quality to which it refers are ambiguous. The act is painfully pleasant to Eve, gratifying to Adam, and morally praiseworthy to the poet; and "sweet" describes either the combination, or any element in the combination, of modesty, desire, and hesitation.

This picture of Adam and Eve concludes with a reference to their naked innocence and the joining of their hands; the latter detail suggests the unity and fidelity of the marriage bond:

> So pass'd they naked on, nor shunn'd the sight
> Of God or Angel, for they thought no ill:
> So hand in hand they pass'd, the loveliest pair
> That ever since in love's imbraces met.
>
> (IV.319–22)

Such passages as these embody conventional formulas of matrimonial harmony in a context that is far from conventional. Milton has subsumed the metaphor of the vine, for instance, within the far more elaborate metaphor of the hair, by which he can focus a variety of contrasts. And the physical characteristics, demeanor, and gestures of Adam and Eve become emblematic not only of the hierarchy of marriage but of the whole marriage ideal; Milton is able to include in the description refinements of tone and complexities of response rarely dealt with in the tracts. Finally, the description has a keen dramatic and ironic relevance because it is Satan who confronts this vision of the ideal.

The irony is furthered in the subsequent joyful conversation between Adam and Eve (IV.411–91). Satan learns of the prohibition of the Tree of Knowledge by which they will be destroyed; but the subtler irony is that Eve's words to Adam echo Sin's declaration of kinship to Satan:

> O thou for whom
> And from whom I was form'd flesh of thy flesh,
> And without whom am to no end, my Guide
> And Head.
>
> (IV.440–43)

Both Eve and Sin mention their origin within their masters and their subservience to them; Satan's consciousness of the differences between Sin and Eve would be no stronger than at this moment of accidental contact. But Eve's speech, along with the

account of her creation, continues Milton's presentation of the
hierarchical order of marriage. Eve declares that she was made
for man ("without whom [I] am to no end"), and that she is not
equal to Adam, "Preeminent by so much odds" (IV.447); both
ideas are significant repetitions of conventional opinions central to Milton's own divorce tracts.

Eve's account of her creation (IV.449–91) is often thought to
be evidence of Eve's inclination to vanity—a critical opinion at
which Marjorie Nicolson takes considerable umbrage.[3] Miss
Nicolson argues that if Eve is inclined toward vanity, then she
was created with a fault, a manifest impossibility in Milton's
theological and dramatic system. This argument is not entirely
sound. The natures of man and woman being somewhat different, it is possible that Milton means to show that they are exposed to different dangers. The danger is not in itself a fault,
any more than a temptation is a sin. Eve's inclination to vanity
is not a weakness of her nature; it is a consequence of the fact
that she is the more immediately attractive of the two creatures.
Vanity simply presents a greater temptation to woman than to
man. In a similar way, Adam's inclination toward sexual passion, toward uxoriousness, is not a fault of his nature but a sign
of his masculinity; this special temptation is one which he
through the exercise of his reason is strong enough to overcome.
Miss Nicolson is right, however, in asserting that Eve's vanity
is not the focal issue of Eve's account. Milton seems to be emphasizing, rather, certain differences between Adam and Eve,
man and woman. First of all, Eve is the more strikingly graceful
of the two; Adam, on first sight, is superficially "less fair,/
Less winning soft, less amiably mild" (IV.478–79). Second, Eve is the
weaker in intelligence and courage. Adam frightens her easily,
and she judges him by his appearance rather than by the wisdom
which it takes her a little time to see. Third, Eve can ultimately
recognize a superior kind of beauty in Adam, a beauty in which
he is superior to her:

3. Marjorie Nicolson, *John Milton: A Reader's Guide to His Poetry* (New
York, 1963), p. 242.

> beauty is excell'd by manly grace
> And wisdom, which alone is truly fair.
>
> (IV.490–91)

The distinction in intellectual powers and uses is an argument for male authority in Milton: Eve is the image of Adam, as Adam is the image of God (IV.471–72); and Eve will say to Adam, "God is thy Law, thou mine: to know no more/ Is woman's happiest knowledge and her praise" (IV.637–38). Finally, Eve's account enables her to acknowledge Adam's love; Milton uses the reference to Adam's rib precisely as the matrimonial writers do—as an indication of union, intimacy, affection, and equality. Adam, she says, cried to her as she returned to the pool:

> Return fair Eve,
> Whom fli'st thou? Whom thou fli'st, of him thou art,
> His flesh, his bone; to give thee being I lent
> Out of my side to thee, nearest my heart
> Substantial Life, to have thee by my side
> Henceforth an individual solace dear;
> Part of my Soul I seek thee, and thee claim
> My other half.
>
> (IV.481–88)

Milton's Adam in this speech emphasizes their union: "of him thou art," "out of my side," "nearest my heart," "by my side," "individual," "part of my soul," "my other half." As the matrimonial writers advise, the affection which proceeds from their singleness gains Eve's obedience to Adam; he seizes Eve with "gentle hand," and Eve "yields" (IV.488–89).

Milton culminates his description of marriage as an expression of ideal order in the scene of Adam and Eve's retirement. Satan has wandered off, to return later in the form of a toad whispering at the ear of Eve; he no longer provides a dramatic focus for this scene. But this relaxation of suspense has a dramatic necessity of its own; Milton wishes to make Adam and Eve the exclusive center of interest for a moment. At this point their relationship, soon to change, is presented at its most ideal. The earlier scene had demonstrated not so much the ideal of human happiness as its frailty; the whole scene had been framed by Satan's presence and his self-absorbed commentary on it: all good is to become his prey, all potential weakness his weapon. But now the sense of danger is diminished, and the paradisal amity of Adam and Eve is shown in its perfection as a symbol of cosmic order.

Book IV of *Paradise Lost* refers to two external signs of human reason and dignity: labor and love. Both of these are proper only to man. Man's appointed labor is evidence of "the regard of Heav'n on all his ways" (IV.620), and the poet hymns wedded love as the rational foundation of domestic life:

> Hail wedded Love, mysterious Law, true source
> Of human offspring, sole propriety
> In Paradise of all things common else.
> By thee adulterous lust was driv'n from men
> Among the bestial herds to range, by thee
> Founded in Reason, Loyal, Just, and Pure,
> Relations dear, and all the Charities
> Of Father, Son, and Brother first were known.
>
> (IV.750–57)

Within the context of this passage, Milton declares marriage pure, as the matrimonial writers had declared it "honorable" (IV.744–47). He sees marriage as a command fulfilling the creative will of God and perverse abstinence as belonging to the devil (IV.748–49), just as the Protestant theologians had condemned vows of virginity. Marriage is the proper sphere of love; Milton celebrates the necessary connection which the divorce tracts had made explicit. He condemns sex without love as he had condemned marriage without love:

> Here Love his golden shafts imploys, here lights
> His constant Lamp, and waves his purple wings,
> Reigns here and revels; not in the bought smile
> Of Harlots, loveless, joyless, unindear'd,
> Casual fruition, nor in Court Amours,

Mixt Dance, or wanton Mask, or Midnight Ball,
Or Serenate, which the starv'd Lover sings
To his proud fair, best quitted with disdain.

(IV.763–70)

Milton creates in the hut to which Adam and Eve retire, the
place of their nuptials (IV.710–14), the perfect symbol of the
holy uniqueness of their love. The place is never entered by the
lower creatures (IV.703–05); its natural beauty, as opposed to
the artificial pomp of a building like Pandemonium, is suggested by the use of architectural terms to describe vegetable
forms (e.g. "roof," "fenc'd up," "wall," "Mosaic," "inlay,"
IV.692–703); and it surpasses in shade, holiness, and secrecy the
bowers in which mythological creatures of uncontrolled sexual
appetite—Pan, Silvanus, and Faunus—diverted themselves
(IV.705–08). Matrimonial love, like the hut which houses it,
is proper to man alone.

The fourth book of *Paradise Lost* in fact gives to marriage
itself a special symbolic importance. Marriage reflects the sensuousness and order of the Garden itself; it is a parallel ideal of
nature; it is a sign of the full humanity of man, of his reason,
will, emotions, and appetites operating in harmony; and it is
the culmination and epitome of human happiness. Books V
through VII of *Paradise Lost* are, on these issues, not highly
elaborative. However, in Book V the mutual affection and unity
of Adam and Eve account for endearing epithets, such as "Heav-
en's last best gift, my ever new delight," "Best image of myself
and dearer half," "My Glory, my Perfection" (V.19, 95, 29). But
this affection is demonstrated particularly in the spiritual encouragement, a form of matrimonial aid, given by Adam to
Eve. Eve recounts to Adam the dream which Satan had inspired,
a dream which foreshadows the actual temptation scene in its
appeals to vanity, curiosity, and ambition; the conclusion of the
dream, in fact, demonstrates the paradox that ambition, like
pride, falls as it hoped to rise. Adam assures Eve that she is not
culpable; he explains the hierarchy of reason, fancy, and sense;
the imitation of reason by "mimic fancy" in dreams; and the

fact that the will alone can produce guilt. Such an explanation is a fulfillment of Adam's matrimonial role as sustainer of his wife in times of moral stress; his understanding and his assurances lend courage to Eve, who is fearful of having sinned. The couple join in mutual prayer before their bower, as they had prayed the night before, and this exercise of piety, like their work, reflects the mutuality of all their virtues and obligations. The work itself, as Milton describes it, involves objects symbolizing male strength and need, female weakness and fertility —the elm and the vine:

> they led the Vine
> To wed her Elm: she spous'd about him twines
> Her marriageable arms, and with her brings
> Her dow'r th' adopted Clusters, to adorn
> His barren leaves.
>   (V.215–19)

These domestic details are further elaborated by one minor episode. When Raphael approaches their bower and Adam asks Eve to bring to the table abundant goods from their larder, Eve, with an instinct for household economy far surer than Adam's, declares that there is no need in Paradise to store anything except foods which improve with storing. She then goes to the garden to gather fruits whose tastes complement one another (V.313–49). Obviously Milton wishes to show some natural superiority of Eve over Adam in the management and disposition of household goods. Eve's domestic nature, outlined here, will be given pathetic overtones later, as the couple prepare to leave the Garden.

Milton's account of the process of creation in Book VII rests on a theory of physical attraction and repulsion, sympathy and antipathy, which receives psychological application in the divorce tracts. Sent out by the Father, the Son creates the world with the assistance of the Holy Spirit by rationally dividing and joining the warring atoms of chaos according to their natures; the Spirit of God first infused the elements with life, separating from them

The black tartareous cold Infernal dregs
Adverse to life; then founded, then conglob'd
Like things to like, the rest to several place
Disparted.

(VII.238–41)

In the divorce tracts, such a process of division and conjunction also characterizes the God of marriage law. In *Paradise Lost,* the "divorce" of unlike elements is creative, just as the continued marriage of unfit partners is, in the divorce tracts, unnatural and destructive, and divorce is thus a part of God's universal law. To anyone who reads this account of the creation with Milton's divorce tractates in mind, marriage and divorce fall into place as a further manifestation of the divine Reason which created the universe.

But Raphael emphasizes another aspect of marriage in his references to Eve—the fertility associated with the wife as vine. He addresses Eve as "Mother of Mankind" (V.388–91), and he speaks to Adam of her creation thus summarily, not having been present at it, as we learn later:

Male he created thee, but thy consort
Female for Race.

(VII.529–30)

Raphael tends to be the spokesman of the view that the wife was created expressly to bear children. But Eve's role is far more complex to Adam, as the prime purpose of marriage was far different to the Milton of the divorce tracts. And Adam will present to Raphael in Book VIII the emotional needs which marriage satisfies, needs not merely human but angelic, and shared by Raphael himself.

Eve's retirement to her garden when Adam and Raphael begin to argue teleology (VIII.39–63) is one of those places in *Paradise Lost* best illuminated by a consciousness of the seventeenth-century ideal of matrimony and of Milton's special refinement of this in the divorce tracts. Milton is careful to indicate that Eve's intellect is not unable to understand and enjoy:

> Yet went she not, as not with such discourse
> Delighted, or not capable her ear
> Of what was high: such pleasure she reserv'd,
> *Adam* relating, she sole Auditress:
> Her Husband the Relater she preferr'd
> Before the Angel, and of him to ask
> Chose rather: hee, she knew, would intermix
> Grateful digressions, and solve high dispute
> With conjugal Caresses, from his Lip
> Not Words alone pleas'd her.
>
> (VIII 48-57)

Eve's withdrawal emphasizes not only the conventionally ideal wifely qualities of retirement (modesty before guests) and fidelity (preference for the husband's company), but also the Miltonic concepts of "fitness" and marital "conversation." Eve is a fit wife (here *fit* in a generic sense) for Adam because she herself desires just the sort of "conversation" which Adam as a husband would seek and desire in her company—the "free and lightsom" intellectual and physical exchange proper to husband and wife. Milton is, in fact, underscoring the distinction between friendship and love by contrasting the "grave" intellectual conversation between Adam and Raphael and the "amiable and attractive" conversation which Eve looks forward to between Adam and herself—a less severe, more intimate dialogue in which "conversation" as we understand it is only a part.

Adam desires from Eve precisely what Eve desires to give to him; and the later parts of Book VIII examine in some detail the objects, felicities, and dangers of Adam's desire. Milton's Adam is by nature a Protestant Adam in being so emphatically marital. Lines 354 to 451 of Book VIII consist of Adam's complaint of dissatisfaction with his solitude, and the Creator's pleased acknowledgment that Adam should recognize his need for a mate. In this long colloquy, God toys gently with Adam as He tests Adam's reason. God is pleased that Adam should find God's answers unsatisfactory; Adam's reason and self-awareness supply the rejoinders that the animals are not a fit answer to his

need of companionship because they are not human, and that
man needs a human companion because he is not wholly perfect, like God, "But in degree": man needs "conversation with
his like to help,/ or Solace his defects."
Each detail in this conversation grows out of attitudes already examined in the matrimonial writers. One attitude is the
implied rejection of the theory held by the Neoplatonist writers
that Adam before the Fall was androgynous, that is, that he
needed no companion except "Wisdom"—already a part of his
nature. The cabalists claimed that when Adam's desire imbruted
—or became physical—God created a woman for him, but Adam
had already fallen in desiring a physical mate.[4] The exchange
of σοφία for Eve was merely the sign of Adam's Fall. But unlike
Marvell's "happy man" in the earthly heaven of "The Garden"
—a poem influenced by Neoplatonist theory—Milton's Adam
does not believe "Two paradises 't were in one/ To live in
Paradise alone," for Adam has neither physical nor spiritual serenity without a companion. Adam's need is part of his created
nature—not a fault, but a necessity of his being man rather than
God. Furthermore, the matrimonial writers' condemnation of
imposed and obligatory virginity for some, when marriage was
"honorable in all," underlies Milton's presentation of Adam's
restlessness. Catholics were not disposed to deny that matrimony
was natural, but they did consider virginity a holier condition
than matrimony, and celibacy a requirement of holy orders. But
Milton's Adam needs Eve's solace, spiritually as well as physi-
cally. In Adam's desire, approved as well as satisfied by God,
Milton rejects both the theory of Adam's androgyny and the
Catholic overvaluation of virginity. The holiness of marriage
was established for all time in the Garden of Eden by God's
sanction and design.

4. See Henry More, *The Philosophick Cabbala*, in *A Collection of Several
Philosophical Writings of Dr. Henry More* (London, 1712-13), 2, pp. 19-20.
See also Jakob Boehme, *Of the Election of Grace*, in *The Works of Jacob
Behmen, Teutonic Theosopher*, trans. William Law (London, 1764-81), 4,
pp. 192-93.

Adam emphasizes his solitude as an argument for the creation of Eve, as Raphael had tended to emphasize procreation. But he mentions both as the purpose of marriage, just as the handbooks of courtesy and matrimony had considered these ends proper to marriage before the Fall, and the remedy of fornication a subsidiary end proper to marriage only after the Fall. It is obvious that Adam's loneliness and desire for help are primary; this is the repeated complaint, and it significantly precedes mention of generation in Milton's text:

> In solitude
> What happiness, who can enjoy alone,
> Or all enjoying, what contentment find?
>
> (VIII.364–66)
>
> Thou in thyself art perfect, and in thee
> Is no deficience found; not so is Man,
> But in degree, the cause of his desire
> By conversation with his like to help
> Or solace his defects. No need that thou
> Shouldst propagate, already infinite;
> And through all numbers absolute, though One;
> But Man by number is to manifest
> His single inperfection, and beget
> Like of his like, his Image multipli'd,
> In unity defective, which requires
> Collateral love, and dearest amity.
>
> (VIII.415–26)

In this recapitulation of the ends of marriage, there are, then, both conventional and distinctive elements: two ends are mentioned, as they are in Genesis and in the matrimonial writers, but one end is given special prominence, emphasizing a priority which Milton felt existed in Genesis, in nature, and in the divine plan. As C. S. Lewis and Balachandre Rajan have pointed out,[5] there is a certain necessary conventionality in *Paradise*

5. C. S. Lewis, *A Preface to Paradise Lost* (London, 1942), pp. 81–91. Balachandre Rajan, *"Paradise Lost" and the Seventeenth Century Reader* (London, 1947), pp. 9–38.

Lost; in the poem, Milton is obliged to underplay heterodox opinions. Even when these occur and are presented as "truth," they are hardly noticed by the reader, who is conscious of reading epic poetry, not theological polemics. Here the slight, rather personal, emphasis upon marriage as a "help" or "solace" is almost inconspicuous; this end, as Milton had pointed out, was given first mention in the Bible and, besides, Milton does not here or elsewhere ignore the second end.

Perhaps a more significant example of the lack of emphasis upon idiosyncratic opinion occurs in the passage in which Adam argues that the company of animals will not completely satisfy him. Milton gives Adam an argument and a vocabulary which he himself had used in the divorce tracts; but in *Paradise Lost* the argument takes place in a far more conventional context. Whereas Milton had used it to declare the unfitness of marriages between certain human beings, Adam uses it merely to point out the impropriety of human "conversation" between man and beast:

> Among unequals what society
> Can sort, what harmony or true delight?
> Which must be mutual, in proportion due
> Giv'n and receiv'd; but in disparity
> The one intense, the other still remiss
> Cannot well suit with either; but soon prove
> Tedious alike: Of fellowship I speak
> Such as I seek, fit to participate
> All rational delight, wherein the brute
> Cannot be human consort.
>
> (VIII.383–92)

If one were to substitute "unfit woman" (or "image of earth and phlegm") for "brute" in the quoted passage, one would have Milton's whole argument for the divorce of "unmeet" partners in summary. But it is a characteristic of Milton's artistic conscience that he does not make *Paradise Lost* in its larger plan a vehicle for personal opinions. His epic universe is Ptolemaic, whatever his own leanings may have been, and in the great astronomical debate of Book VIII the Copernican system, which he may have favored, is argued only with the greatest cautions and qualifications. The rhetorical situation being different, the opinions and referents change even as the situation does. Milton here uses the vocabulary of the divorce tracts but not the ideas. Like Milton's heterodox theology, which cannot be fitted into the poetry without much pulling and tugging, his heterodox matrimonial views stand apart from the poem, and when they appear they are tempered and altered by the context. It would be a grave error to read some of the opinions of the divorce tracts into *Paradise Lost,* as Maurice Kelley has read the theological opinions into it,[6] except to illustrate how subdued his heterodoxy becomes within the epic. For both the private speculation of *De Doctrina Christiana* and the public argument of the divorce tracts differ from the public faith of *Paradise Lost.*

Yet the language and the conceptions of the poem with respect to the creation of Eve correspond in many minor ways to those of the divorce tracts. Phrases like "collateral love," "dearest amity," "social communication," and the technical "complacence" (VIII.426, 429, 433) identify what Adam seeks in marriage, just as they are precisely the essence of marriage according to Milton's divorce tracts. And when God declares His intention of creating a mate for Adam, He does so with a predictable emphasis upon words denoting likeness, fitness, and meetness (VIII.442, 448). Eve is created, He tells Adam,

> Thy likeness, thy fit help, thy other self,
> Thy wish, exactly to thy heart's desire.

> (VIII.450–51)

Words such as these express the perfection of the union and consonance of Adam and Eve; they grow out of the long tradition that their marriage was the perfect pattern and archetype of all marriages.

6. Maurice Kelley, *This Great Argument: A Study of Milton's* De Doctrina Christiana *as a Gloss upon* Paradise Lost (Princeton, 1941).

God puts Adam to sleep, but through his fancy He allows him to see the creation of Eve. The motif so frequently sounded in Book IV reappears; Eve epitomizes for Adam all the delights of this world:

> Under his forming hands a Creature grew,
> Manlike, but different sex, so lovely fair,
> That what seem'd fair in all the World, seem'd now
> Mean, or in her summ'd up, in her contain'd
> And in her looks, which from that time infus'd
> Sweetness into my heart, unfelt before,
> And into all things from her Air inspir'd
> The spirit of love and amorous delight.
>
> (VIII.470–77)

This passage, with its intricate patterns of resonance—"seem'd," "seem'd," "summ'd"; "manlike," "mean"; repetitions in different contexts of "fair" and "in her"; the consonance of "f" and "s" sounds; and the subtle etymological similarities of "Air," "inspir'd," and "spirit," and "love" and "amorous"—is a joyful celebration of the birth of human love. Adam despairs when he wakes to find the vision gone; but the real Eve reappears before him, led by God and indeed summing up both heaven and earth:

> Grace was in all her steps, Heavn in her Eye,
> In every gesture dignity and love.
>
> (VIII.488–89)

Adam declares himself and Eve "individual" (as the marriage writers would say): "they shall be one Flesh, one Heart, one Soul." This declaration is followed by Eve's hesitation, a hesitation explained somewhat differently by Eve in Book IV and by Adam in Book VIII. Eve's explanation has the overtones of weakness (vanity, fear, lack of understanding) as well as the more favorable implication of modesty. Adam emphasizes Eve's natural impulse to retirement and her consciousness of dignity and equality:

> She heard me thus, and though divinely brought,
> Yet Innocence and Virgin Modesty,
> Her virtue and the conscience of her worth,
> That would be woo'd, and not unsought be won,
> Not obvious, not obtrusive, but retir'd,
> The more desirable.
>
> (VIII.500–05)

This combination of modesty and reluctance is overcome by Adam; and the quality of Eve's submission, that of one equal in the possession of reason and superior in the possession of beauty, is characterized by the paradox "obsequious Majesty" (VIII.509).

The final section of Book VII concerns the propriety of love —in Adam, in the angels, and in God's plan. The love of Adam for Eve has its special dangers, which Raphael sedulously warns Adam against. Adam declares that his passion for Eve seems to be a weakness in his nature (VIII.530–39). He realizes that Eve combines superior beauty with inferior mental faculties, "in outward show/ Elaborate, of inward less exact" (VIII.538–39), yet he finds himself awed and submissive before her:

> when I approach
> Her loveliness, so absolute she seems
> And in herself complete, so well to know
> Her own, that what she wills to do or say,
> Seems wisest, virtuousest, discreetest, best;
> All higher knowledge in her presence falls
> Degraded, Wisdom in discourse with her
> Loses discount'nanc't, and like folly shows;
> Authority and Reason on her wait,
> As one intended first, not after made
> Occasionally; and to consummate all,
> Greatness of mind and nobleness thir seat
> Build in her loveliest, and create an awe
> About her, as a guard Angelic plac't.
>
> (VIII.546–59)

Marjorie Nicolson takes this passage as Milton's tribute to woman,[7] but it is obvious, from the speech itself and from the context, that Milton intends another response. There is no doubt of the compelling and attractive power of the verse; the passage does express the keen exaltation of human passion. Like many another tribute to woman, the language is hyperbolic; but the danger is that the hyperbole is too near actual delusion. Adam inverts the whole order of nature in according superiority to Eve: her desire and speech are *not* by nature "wisest, virtuousest, discreetest, best"; they only have the power to *seem* so because of her beauty. In Adam's tribute, all superior rights and faculties lose their place in the natural order: "higher knowledge," "Wisdom," "Authority and Reason." "Her loveliest" becomes the seat of "greatness of mind and nobleness" in an obvious distortion of the appropriate relationship. Two misfortunes are implied by this process; man has lost the power to distinguish the worthy from the less worthy, and, as a result of this loss of reason, he has lost the right to rule. As the matrimonial writers would put it, obedience belongs only to him who can exercise his power of reason; otherwise he forfeits his authority to the wife.

Raphael replies to Adam's assertions "with contracted brow." His displeasure and concern issue in a series of cautions to Adam: he asserts the perfection of nature in Adam, who is nonetheless responsible for self-control; the superiority of reality over appearance, reason over beauty, and male authority over female attractiveness (VIII.561–94). The whole argument advises Adam to realize that he is superior to Eve and must remain conscious of that fact to maintain his authority. Like the matrimonial writers, Raphael declares that Adam's authority rests upon the right estimate of things:

> Oft-times nothing profits more
> Than self-esteem, grounded on just and right
> Well-manag'd; of that skill the more thou know'st,

7. Nicolson, *John Milton*, p. 278.

The more she will acknowledge thee her Head,
And to realities yield all her shows.

                                        (VIII.571–75)

Raphael advises Adam that carnality is common to the animals,
that Adam should love the proper object in Eve ("What higher
in her society thou find'st/ Attractive, human, rational, love
still," IV.586–87), and that love has an object beyond woman:
human love "is the scale/ By which to heavenly Love thou
may'st ascend" (IV 591–92). At this point Milton has Adam re-
fine upon some of Raphael's judgments and even turn back
some of his arguments upon him. Adam, to be sure, is "half-
abash't" at the angel's warning and tone, but he claims that the
act of "the genial Bed" is different in its manner and its mystery
from the act of procreation "common to all kinds" (IV.596–99),
and he defends himself by claiming that he is most delighted by
other aspects of his "conversation" with Eve:

                    those graceful acts,
        Those thousand decencies that daily flow
        From all her words and actions, mixt with Love
        And sweet compliance, which declare unfeign'd
        Union of Mind, or in us both one Soul;
        Harmony to behold in wedded pair
        More grateful than harmonious sound to the ear.
                                        (VIII.600–06)

What Adam loves in Eve is precisely that disposition to union
which Milton had considered essential to marriage in the divorce tracts. It is the feminine in Eve that he loves, not merely
the female. The "acts of peace and love" celebrated in the tracts
as the expression of matrimonial compatibility are the strongest
attraction Eve can exert upon Adam. Terms such as "compliance," "union of Mind," and "harmony" echo the standards set
forward in the prose tracts: the wife's necessary disposition toward obedience, the sense of spiritual oneness which included
for Milton more than the conventional "matrimonial consent,"

and the frequent musical analogies. These lines demonstrate, furthermore, that the ideal marriage between Adam and Eve has not been static; Adam's love for Eve at her creation has increased through knowledge of her spiritual beauty and her "fitness." But the chief bond between this passage and Milton's tracts is the emphasis upon the spirituality of love. As Milton had argued against opponents who considered adultery the chief violation of marriage by maintaining that the clash of temperament involved a more essential rupture, he here celebrates the sense of unity produced by a consonance of feeling and will. Adam proves his "judicious" love by loving what in Eve is worthiest, the "Love/And sweet compliance" expressed in her acts. Adam says, however, that even Eve's 'graceful acts" do not "subject" him; that he can distinguish among various goods and approve the best, as the angel had advised him:

> In loving thou dost well, in passion not,
> Wherein true love consists not; Love refines
> The thoughts, and heart enlarges, hath his seat
> In Reason, and is judicious, is the scale
> By which to heavenly Love thou may'st ascend,
> Not sunk in carnal pleasure, for which cause
> Among the Beasts no Mate for thee was found.
>
> (VIII.588–94)

Adam, as rationally acute with Raphael in discussing love as he had been with God in begging a mate, turns the question of love back upon the angel. Raphael is obliged to admit both that love exists among the angels and that it involves a form of union (VIII.618–29). But he ends the colloquy with a well-placed warning.

The discussion of love in Book VIII complicates the Fall a great deal. There is no doubt that Adam falls through uxoriousness, "fondly overcome with female charm," but the uxoriousness is not passion in the usual sense of excessive sexual love of the wife. Not the specifically sexual charms of Eve but rather her human, submissive, feminine qualities overpower Adam's

reason. For Adam loves in Eve precisely what the angel tells
him to. One of the central paradoxes of *Paradise Lost* is that
Milton has so constructed his argument that it is exactly the
perfection of his marriage with Eve which acts upon Adam as
the greatest incentive to succumb to the temptation to disobey.
But Adam's love for Eve—high, noble, and well justified in itself—does become, at the moment of the Fall, passion. It is
passion not in the sense of uncontrolled sexual desire but in the
sense of an excessive desire for human love. In the act of disobedience, Adam simply chooses Eve over God; he rejects human love as a means and deifies it as an end.

It was precisely this choice that Raphael warned Adam
against:

> Be strong, live happy, and love, but first of all
> Him whom to love is to obey, and keep
> His great command; take heed lest Passion sway
> Thy judgment to do aught, which else free Will
> Would not admit.
>
> (VIII.633–37)

Here, then, Raphael allows the love of Eve to Adam, but that
love exists in a hierarchy of attitudes, chief of which is love of
God, expressing itself in obedience to Him. Milton does not
sentimentalize the love relationship of Adam and Eve by giving
it any absolute value. Human love merely has a place in a hierarchy, below the values of order, obedience, and spiritual love.
But Milton does not attempt any account of spiritual love in
Paradise Lost, even though he celebrates matrimonial love with
candid fervor. When Raphael and Adam discuss the mysteries
of the universe, they discuss astronomy and physics, not the
soul's relationship to God. The coolness and detachment of
Milton's God (somewhat mitigated, to be sure, by the charity
and ardor of the Son) is matched by the absence in *Paradise Lost*
of any elaborate discussion of the mystical way or of spiritual
ascent through love. At the moment when Raphael defines the
place of spiritual love in the order of nature, Milton might well

have done what he had done with matrimonial love, but he shuns an opportunity which Dante might have handsomely exploited.

Instead, Milton has emphasized the ethical implications of Adam's love for Eve. The Angel unequivocally denies that Adam is imperfect. Adam's uxoriousness is a potential fault, but it is not actual, any more than is Eve's vanity. To admit the special possibility of uxoriousness in Adam or of vanity in Eve does not argue a defect in either; their very nature as free beings must always admit the possibility of sin, whether through uxoriousness, vanity, or something else. Adam's tendency toward uxoriousness is merely a special danger of his being masculine. By the end of Book VIII Raphael has given Adam three warnings: Satan is subtle, Adam must not succumb to passion, and Adam must maintain authority over Eve. The Fall, when it occurs, involves the deliberate neglect of all three, and the particular corruption of married order.

Book IX makes the matrimonial relationship one of the instruments and reflectors of man's Fall, as Book X makes it one of the aids to his salvation. Adam's Fall is the dramatic turning point of *Paradise Lost;* and marriage is directly involved in Milton's presentation of the act in two ways. First, the Fall occurs when Adam allows passion to dominate reason; that is, when he decides that his love for Eve is more important than his obedience to God. An internal corruption of this kind is also a disruption of the matrimonial hierarchy. Adam, having allowed the lesser good to outweigh the greater, has forfeited his right to authority. Eve assumes the dominant role in persuading Adam to evil. Secondly, the effects of the Fall are first dramatized in the corruption of their marriage. Brutal sensuality rather than "amiable conversation" characterizes their lovemaking, and their passion, indulged to excess, produces weariness and surfeit. Having slept, they fall to quarreling and mutual recrimination. Book IX, therefore, focuses the central act of disobedience through the relationship of Adam and Eve.

The scene of separation before the Fall (IX.205–411) begins as

a debate on household economy but expands to an argument
on virtue. Eve wants a separation in order to work more ef-
ficiently. The responses of Adam and Eve are in both parts of
the debate typical of their sex. The opposition between Eve's
practicality and Adam's desire for her company establishes a
different degree of concern for household matters. When the
debate enlarges its issues through Adam's mention of the special
danger of Satan, Eve's response is a charming mixture of feminine indignation, wounded affection, and careful self-control
(IX.269–71). Eve wins the debate because Adam recognizes her
freedom to do as she likes in matters in themselves of moral
indifference.

Adam's culpability in allowing Eve to part from him is
claimed by Eve herself after the Fall has occurred. The charge,
however, is then obviously an attempt at self-exculpation. Adam
wants her to remain with him, and his decision to allow her to
leave, considered in itself, would not seem ill advised to any
reader of matrimonial handbooks. Eve's lack of prudence rather
than Adam's lack of insistence seems to make the Fall possible.
Adam's love for Eve does not neutralize his right to demand
obedience, and he is not in fact guilty of uxoriousness. He is
rightly showing his love for her in not forcing her to remain; he
is exercising his authority with love and gentleness.

Throughout the debate, Adam's matrimonial solicitude is
evident, expressed in terms which suggest the special moral
strength of marriage and the mutual watchfulness of the effort
toward piety and virtue (IX.267–69, 309–17, 357–58, 367–69).
In his warnings to Eve, Adam assumes the role which Raphael
had had with respect to him. He is especially careful to point
out the relationship between reason and will and the danger of
misapprehended good (IX.351–56). In all this, Eve rather than
Adam has the less cogent arguments. Eve's use of the generalizations of *Areopagitica* ("what is Faith, Love, Virtue unassay'd/
Alone, without exterior help sustain'd?"—IX.335–36) is properly qualified by Adam's "Trial will come unsought" (IX.366).
Adam does as much to convince Eve as a husband can do, and

his permission for the separation is not a weak yielding of power but a recognition of the capacity for virtue in the wife:

Go; for thy stay, not free, absents thee more;
Go in thy native innocence, rely
On what thou hast of virtue, summon all,
For God towards thee hath done his part, do thine.

(IX.372–75)

Various forms of human love hereafter provide a motif for Milton's account of the Fall. Satan's "seduction" of Eve has obvious sexual overtones.[8] He uses the language of a lover serenading his mistress and begins to win her by an appeal to her vanity:

So gloz'd the Tempter, and his Proem tun'd;
Into the Heart of *Eve* his words made way.

(IX.549–50)

Eve's submission to Satan might be considered a form of infidelity to Adam. But once Eve has fallen, she turns her attention to the question of whether Adam should be allowed to share the fruit of the tree with her. If she keeps her secret, she thinks, it would be possible for her to be his superior; Eve's matrimonial ambition is her first specifically domestic crime. She confuses liberty with license ("inferior who is free?"—IX.825), not realizing that freedom is possible only within one's place in a hierarchy. Mindfulness of the threat of death, however, compels Eve to share her secret with Adam; her motive is jealousy, a perversion of love. If she dies Adam may be given a new mate. It is love, then, but selfish love, love which wishes to possess and if necessary completely destroy its object, which motivates

8. Benjamin Needler cites four reasons for the temptation of Eve rather than Adam by the devil: the strength of Adam's impression of God's prohibition, Eve's frailer nature, the power of Eve over Adam, and Eve's ability to excuse herself if Adam had fallen first. Eve would be no less culpable if tempted by Adam, but she would have been full of words of excuse nonetheless (Needler, *Expository Notes*, p. 64).

Eve to bring about Adam's disobedience to God.⁹ From this
point until the end of Book IX, the word "love" will always
appear in a fairly sinister context and carry an ironic meaning.
For instance, when Eve returns to Adam, she ambiguously says
that she had never felt the "agony of love" until their separation,
and she cunningly uses love as an argument in tempting Adam:

> Thou therefore also taste, that equal Lot
> May join us, equal Joy, as equal Love.

(IX.881–82)

Adam's inward soliloquy, which follows, contains no particular
conflict; Eve's Fall, Adam seems to feel, has determined his
own. Love is his motive, but it is a love which subverts the order
of nature. Yet there is enormous pathos in the attraction Adam
feels toward Eve:

> I feel
> The Link of Nature draw me: Flesh of my Flesh,
> Bone of my Bone thou art, and from thy State
> Mine never shall be parted, bliss or woe.

(IX.913–16)

The repetition of the words which emphasize the indissolubi-
lity of marriage, used at the creation of Eve and referred to
continually by matrimonial writers, here lends a kind of fatality
to the tragic act, and for a moment we see Adam as helpless before the power of conjugal love:

> if Death
> Consort with thee, Death is to mee as Life;
> So forcible within my heart I feel
> The Bond of Nature draw me to my own,

9. Eve's rather complicated reasoning is Milton's means of dramatizing
human corruption after the Fall. Benjamin Needler, for instance, does not
think that Eve intended either to deceive or to injure Adam (Needler, p. 81).
John Brinsley also thinks of Eve primarily as a victim of Satan's deception,
not as a deceiver herself (A Looking-Glasse for Good Women [London,
1645], pp. 2–6).

My own in thee, for what thou art is mine;
Our State cannot be sever'd, we are one,
One flesh; to lose thee were to lose myself.

(IX.953–59)

But this tragic decision involves a double irony: Adam's values
have become inverted, so that his "love" is no longer love by
Raphael's definition, and Eve, for whose love he makes his
sacrifice, is impelled by the basest motives, concealed by her
words. The ironic implications of the word "love" are nowhere
so evident as in Eve's apostrophe to Adam (IX.960–89), where
the repetition of the word (IX.961, 970, 975, 983) underscores
the deceptions, external and internal, implicit in Adam's Fall.
Eve lies about her own feelings (IX.979–81), and might better
have described Adam's love as excess, passion, uxoriousness, or
disobedience—a complex violation of the internal, domestic,
and cosmic hierarchies.[10] At the end of Eve's apostrophe, when
the poet resumes the narrative, words such as "love," "ennobl'd,"
"recompense," and "merits" are ironic reflections of Eve's point
of view, and the poet's consciousness of the inversion of roles (as
Adam submits to Eve's authority) is demonstrated by his ironic
use of "compliance," a term proper to domestic treatises:

So saying, she embrac'd him, and for joy
Tenderly wept, much won that he his Love
Had so ennobl'd, as of choice to incur
Divine displeasure for her sake, or Death.

10. Charles Broxolme also attributes to one act a number of sins, although
they are rather different from Milton's analysis of specific motives:
  And further, do but see what a company of sins it containes, and therefore
  it is called *the fall*, it being not one sin, but many: As 1. *Infidelity*, our first
  parents doubting of the truth of divine threatning. 2. *Idolatry*, They be-
  leeving the Divel more then God. 3. *Horrible unthankfulnesse*, They con-
  ceiting God to envy their good estate. 4. *Curiosity*, They affecting more
  knowledg then God had allotted them. 5. *Intolerable pride and ambition:*
  they desiring to be equal with God. 6. *Murder*, both of themselves, and
  whole posterity.
The good Old Way (London, 1653), p. 84.

> In recompense (for such compliance bad
> Such recompense best merits) from the bough
> She gave him of that fair enticing fruit
> With liberal hand: he scrupl'd not to eat
> Against his better knowledge, not deceiv'd,
> But fondly overcome with Female charm.
>
> (IX.990–99)

Milton, then, not only uses a sexual metaphor to describe the fall of Eve, but gives us in the Fall of Adam a dramatization of the corruption of marriage. Eve, seduced by Satan, is "deflower'd" by her Fall (IX.901); and as her love becomes jealousy and her obedience is transformed to unwomanly ambition, Adam's love becomes uxoriousness and his authority is reduced to unmanly compliance. This perversion of love and obedience fittingly culminates in a debasement of sexual love. Just as the relationship between Adam and Eve had been considered by them and by Satan the epitome of their bliss, it is now the epitome of their deceptive happiness and a microcosm of the Fall and its disorder:

> hee on *Eve*
> Began to cast lascivious Eyes, she him
> As wantonly repaid; in Lust they burn.
>
> (IX.1013–15)

Adam's repetition of the words "delicious," "delightful," and "pleasure" to describe the taste of the fruit (IX.1017–33) recalls the earlier epithets for the Garden of Eden itself, epithets which characterized the Garden as a place of sensuous pleasure, a pleasure summed up in the marriage of Adam and Eve. But such pleasure was ordered and innocent; man observed his place in the hierarchy by obedience to God, and he maintained control over his lower appetites by the exercise of reason. Love was a fit symbol of the harmony and happiness of internal and external order. But as "amiable conversation" was proper to man's unfallen state, lust is proper to his new condition. Adam, in seizing Eve's hand (IX.1037), summarizes the brutal impatience of lust and lack of control. The image obviously contrasts with the matrimonial joining of hands (IV.489) and the separation of the vinelike Eve from her supporting partner (IX.385–86). Eve, "nothing loath" (IX.1039), has lost her feminine modesty as Adam has lost his gentleness, and their sin is both "sealed" and "solaced" by their sexual act, a merely sensual conversation marked by the overindulgence and intemperance which matrimonial treatises had condemned:

> they thir fill of Love and Love's disport
> Took largely, of thir mutual guilt the Seal,
> The solace of thir sin, till dewy sleep
> Oppress'd them, wearied with thir amorous play.
>
> (IX.1042–45)

In Book IX, matrimony helps further define the results of the Fall in Adam's desire for solitude, the internal distemper which produces the quarrel, the quarrel over responsibility for the Fall, and Adam's long condemnation of Eve. Adam's wish for a solitary life (IX.1084–90) is essentially an expression of his guilt, but it contrasts markedly with his earlier desire for a companion and with his reluctance to part from Eve. Adam and Eve manage to hide their external nakedness, but they fall to weeping; worse storms rise within them, the turbulence of the disordered faculties of understanding, will, and appetite (IX.1121–31), producing

> high Passions, Anger, Hate,
> Mistrust, Suspicion, Discord.
>
> (IX.1123–24)

These work themselves out in Adam's quarrel with Eve and his condemnation of her, which concludes with Adam's matrimonial moral:

> Thus it shall befall
> Him who to worth in Woman overtrusting
> Lets her Will rule; restraint she will not brook,

And left to herself, if evil thence ensue,
Shee first his weak indulgence will accuse.

(IX.1182–86)

Adam's opinion is cynical and overstated, but in the main it
exposes a common view of the domestic hierarchy. However, it
is unfair to woman in not being qualified by a consciousness of
her balancing virtues. The fall of Adam was woman's first crime
not only against man but against household order; and yet, as
Milton demonstrates in Book X, woman is capable of restoring
both.[11]

Book X redeems Eve psychologically. In Book IX she had
been mercilessly exposed as vain, self-centered, and deceitful;
in Book X Adam rather than Eve seems the more reprehensible.
In the scene of judgment, for instance, the Son elicits contrasting responses from Adam and Eve. Adam is eager to find ration-
alizations for laying his blame upon Eve: necessity (which has
been the tyrant Satan's plea), the impossibility of concealment,
his mistaken trust in her. His tone is whining as he seeks to
purge himself of blame; God had given Eve to him as a perfect
gift, and therefore Adam could not suspect her (X.137–43). The
Son answers that Adam had resigned his proper office as husband; he does not blame Adam for having separated from Eve
but for having subjected himself to her will in eating the fruit
of the tree. The Son in his answer uses the matrimonial standards of the tracts and significantly repeats the distinctions of
Raphael's warning:

Was shee thy God, that her thou didst obey
Before his voice, or was shee made thy guide,
Superior, or but equal, that to her
Thou didst resign thy Manhood, and the Place

11. On the question of whose sin was greater, Adam's or Eve's, Needler
says, "it would not have been an easy matter to have determined . . . had
not God done it, as it were to our hands, by inflicting a greater punishment
on *Eve*, then on Adam" (Needler, p. 72). Cornelius Agrippa, of course, believed the opposite (Agrippa, *The Glory of Women*, p. 18).

Wherein God set thee above her made of thee,
And for thee, whose perfection far excell'd
Hers in all real dignity: Adorn'd
She was indeed, and lovely to attract
Thy Love, not thy Subjection, and her Gifts
Were such as under Government well seem'd,
Unseemly to bear rule, which was thy part
And person, hadst thou known thyself aright.

(X.145–56)

By contrast, Eve, unlike Adam and unlike shrewish women, replies with full consciousness of her guilt, "The Serpent me beguil'd and I did eat" (X.162). The simplicity of her manner makes this short self-condemnation an attractive contrast to Adam's long, arrogant self-exculpation. Eve's punishment is further subjection to the authority of her husband, a necessary surrender of her will to his and a fitting sentence for a crime of willful ambition (X.195–96).

The scene of reconciliation between Adam and Eve follows hard upon Adam's soliloquy, in which Adam has recognized his guilt but not found solace for his affliction. He has reached the stage of "conviction of sin" but not those of conversion or confession.[12] The abusive epithets which both Adam and Eve had used in the quarrel of Book IX here culminate in Adam's outburst:

Out of my sight, thou Serpent, that name best
Befits thee with him leagu'd, thyself as false
And hateful; nothing wants, but that thy shape,
Like his, and color Serpentine may show
Thy inward fraud, to warn all Creatures from thee
Henceforth; lest that too heav'nly form, pretended
To hellish falsehood, snare them.

(X.867–73)

This short exclamation concentrates a number of themes and

12. See Nicolson, pp. 303–05.

allusions. To begin with, the very name of Eve was believed a form of the Hebrew word for serpent, *Heva*. The etymology was one which certain Church Fathers such as Clement of Alexandria found useful in pointing out the dangers of womankind. But Adam uses the term to emphasize the fraudulence of Eve's appearance, the apparent fairness which cloaked her real deceptiveness, as the form of the serpent disguised Satan. Eve worked upon Adam the same trick which the Serpent had worked upon her. Beyond this, there is an obvious connection in both image and theme with the figure of Sin, whose torso and lower parts combine beauty with repulsiveness and suggest the disjunction between apparent good and actual evil. However, Adam has forgotten a final, more hopeful connection— the enmity between Serpent and Woman, the bruising of the Serpent's head by her Seed (X.179–81).[13]

Adam's consciousness of Eve's guilt makes him discard the conventional symbology of the rib in favor of a new one:

> a Rib
> Crooked by nature, bent, as now appears,
> More to the part sinister from me drawn,
> Well if thrown out, as supernumerary
> To my just number found.

(X.884–88)

Milton has Adam here adapt the symbol to express his new attitude toward Eve. Originally, the fact that the rib had been near Adam's heart was a sign of his necessary affection for Eve, and the fact that it had been part of his body betokened their indivisibility. Adam now uses the rib as a symbol of nearly opposite

---

13. John Brinsley, who seems to have used the same biblical commentaries as Milton (he too quotes "Henimgius," Erasmus, Beza, and Paraeus; see Brinsley, pp. 1, 4, 15), devotes a long passage to a careful refutation of the notion that feminine counsel after the Fall is to be disregarded (ibid., pp. 42–44). His view of women, like Milton's, is balanced by a consciousness of their power of insight and their capacity for virtue.

ideas: Eve's innate faultiness, her superfluousness, and his rejection of her. The peculiar unmeetness which he sees in her now impels Adam to call the woman he had once declared perfect (to Raphael) "this fair defect/ Of nature" (X.891–92). And he goes on, in language very much like that of Milton discussing choice in the divorce tracts, to declare that unfit marriages will be one of the effects of man's Fall:

> either
> He never shall find out fit Mate, but such
> As some misfortune brings him, or mistake,
> Or whom he wishes most shall seldom gain
> Through her perverseness, but shall see her gain'd
> By a far worse, or if she love, withheld
> By Parents, or his happiest choice too late
> Shall meet, already linkt and Wedlock-bound
> To a fell Adversary, his hate or shame:
> Which infinite calamity shall cause
> To Human life, and household peace confound.
>
> (X.899–908)

Eve wins Adam to her, however, by her meekness and her suggestion of self-sacrifice. She approaches him with "tresses all disorder'd" (X.911), the same tresses which, like the vine, had signified her submissiveness and dependence. Now, without the prop of Adam's comfort and strength, they signify despair. Milton, in fact, makes a visual pun of the word "distress" (X.942). Moved by her humility, her dependence, and once again by her beauty, Adam responds to the need Eve has of him and becomes once again her support, raising her from her helpless position:

> her lowly plight,
> Immovable till peace obtain'd from fault
> Acknowledg'd and deplor'd, in Adam wrought
> Commiseration; soon his heart relented
> Towards her, his life so late and sole delight,

> Now at his feet submissive in distress,
> Creature so fair his reconcilement seeking,
> His counsel whom she had displeas'd, his aid;
> As one disarm'd, his anger all he lost,
> And thus with peaceful words uprais'd her soon.
>
> (X.937–46)

Eve had offered to bear the punishment of both their sins; Adam recognizes the impossibility of her doing so, but, moved by her offer, desires to make the same sacrifice (X.952–57). The act of performing once again the office proper to the husband—protecting and comforting the wife—leads Adam to full repentance. And he could not have acted unless Eve had first recovered qualities proper to the wife—humility, submission, and desire to aid. In the dramatic structure of *Paradise Lost,* this moment, with Adam's change of heart toward Eve, is a new turning point which now directs the action of the human characters toward confession, prayer for God's mercy, and ultimate redemption. Adam, "Immovable till peace obtain'd from fault/Acknowledg'd and deplor'd," changes only because Eve *has* made the acknowledgment. The restoration of matrimonial harmony creates the possibility of a larger harmony between man and God, and Eve's act of peace and love leads to a greater spiritual reconciliation. Once again Eve has become Adam's help, here through recognizing that he is hers.

Once more united, Eve and Adam debate their new course. Eve's womanly suggestions of childlessness or suicide are put down by Adam with superior arguments; at no time does Milton let us forget that Adam is intellectually more gifted and accomplished than Eve. Adam lights upon the solution of repentance; Eve having produced the mood which softened Adam's heart, they both adopt before God the position which Eve had assumed before Adam:

> they forthwith to the place
> Repairing where he judg'd them prostrate fell

Before him reverent, and both confess'd
Humbly thir faults, and pardon begg'd, with tears
Watering the ground, and with thir sighs the Air
Frequenting, sent from hearts contrite, in sign
Of sorrow unfeign'd, and humiliation meek.

(X.1098–1104)

Once reconciled with each other and with God, Adam and
Eve are restored to a new mutual respect. When he rises from
confession, Adam addresses Eve with a title which calls attention to this attitude: *"Eve* rightly call'd, Mother of all Mankind,/ Mother of all things living" (XI.159–60). The etymology
of Eve, "life," which now reinforces the new posture of respect
and love, contrasts with the earlier etymology of "serpent." It
is precisely her role as mother of mankind which will produce
redemption from the Serpent. By this point, Milton has given
us in Eve the portrait of all the matrimonial virtues and vices
which the popular treatises attributed to the wife: her submissiveness, meekness, and household care before the Fall; her vanity, usurpation of authority, and robbery of goods at the time
of the Fall; and her solace and aid to piety after the Fall. Similarly, Adam as husband has gone through the stages of love and
contentment, uxoriousness and loss of authority, displeasure
and alienation, and, finally, reconciliation and respect. Love
itself has been shown to be both sublimating and imbruting,
requiring for its proper use obedience to God.

In Books XI and XII, Milton maintains certain distinctions
between man and woman, although the focus shifts from the
personal drama to the history of mankind. On being told by
the angel that they must leave the Garden, Eve's lament is a
characteristically feminine reaction; she mourns the loss of her
garden, her flowers, and the "nuptial Bower" with the same special concern for the household which had marked her earlier
reactions. Michael, however, in a passage which nearly parallels
his later hopeful assertion to Adam of a "paradise within," says
that Eve in remaining with Adam takes her garden with her:

> Thy going is not lonely, with thee goes
> Thy Husband, him to follow thou art bound;
> Where he abides, think there thy native soil.

(XI.290–92)

This advice seems peculiarly suited to woman. It provides a domestic lesson as opposed to the larger ethical lesson of Adam's vision; and it re-establishes in the new context of the Fall the earlier concept of matrimony as an epitome of the Garden. Having learned the lesson of wifely fidelity, Eve is put to sleep. Adam, who is not only a husband but the father of all mankind, must be given full knowledge of suffering, sin, and death.

In the visions which immediately follow, particular sins which were specifically involved in Original Sin—murder, intemperance, and lust—are brought before Adam in all their horror: he sees the murder of Abel, the lazar house, and the tents of wickedness. They recall specifically Eve's willingness to precipitate Adam's death, their mutual tempting of death through disobedience, Eve's lack of control over her appetite, Adam's uxoriousness, and their subsequent sensuality. The scene and moral of the tents of wickedness have the most obvious relevance to Adam's sin (XI.556–636). The women who tempt the "Sons of God" abuse their womanly qualities as Eve's attractiveness had ensured Adam's disobedience. Adam points the moral that man's woe begins with woman (X.632–33), but Michael redirects the moral to man and emphasizes the theme of internal and domestic hierarchy:

> From man's effeminate slackness it begins,
> ... who should better hold his place
> By wisdom, and superior gifts receiv'd.

(XI.634–36)

But if passages such as this delineate the corruption of man in marriage, others—especially in Book XII—emphasize the role of marriage in bringing forth a Redeemer (XI.232–35, 325

ff., 375–85, 594–605, etc.). And the hopefulness of the final re-
union of Adam and Eve nearly overshadows the darker hints
of their history and future:

> Both in one Faith unanimous though sad,
> With cause for evils past, yet much more cheer'd
> With meditation on the happy end.

> (XII.603–05)

When Eve greets Adam, she expresses the unanimity which the
angel predicts and which Milton had considered the essence of
marriage. Eve is the perfect wife, even for fallen Adam, who is
her Paradise:

> with thee to go,
> Is to stay here; without thee here to stay,
> Is to go hence unwilling; thou to mee
> Art all things under Heav'n, all places thou.

> (XII.615–18)

This unanimity is reflected in the final image of the poem—two
solitary figures in an immense landscape, wandering, as we had
first seen them in Paradise, "hand in hand" (XII.646–49).

God had created the new world of Adam and Eve to compen-
sate for the depletion of heaven by the angelic revolt; when the
earth itself was shattered by human revolt God created another
Paradise, that of interior grace. The final assertion of *Paradise
Lost* is that God's creativity is inexhaustible, adaptable, and
restorative: what is lost He replaces, what is corrupted He
makes new. But marriage has a special place in both the economy of creation and the structure of the poem. The marriage of
Adam and Eve corresponds throughout to their internal dispositions; but something survives disorder and helps to overcome
it—union of husband and wife. At the end of the poem, the restored unanimity of Adam and Eve is a domestic parallel to the
realm of grace and order, the promised "Paradise within." The
Garden symbol, applied to both internal and domestic happi-

ness, establishes the connection. And in the final books of the poem, the relationship between Adam and Eve justifies an even stronger parallel. Eve had sinned; Adam, tempted by her, had fallen through "love." But Eve led him to repentance and through her motherhood would bring forth the Redeemer. Adam's love, therefore, like his disobedience, is a *felix culpa*. The poem as a whole assents to all the conditions of human life and marriage—impermanence, change, and decay—because though lamentable in themselves they can be made part of a higher order of values. This, more than anything, seems implied by the "new" matrimony of Adam and Eve, confronting an unknown world "hand in hand."

Conclusion

Milton's strategy to establish a reform of divorce laws in England moved from argument based on natural reason and Scripture as interpreted by Puritan divines (*Doctrine and Discipline of Divorce*, 1643) to a restatement buttressed by authorities (*Doctrine and Discipline of Divorce*, 1644) to appeal to authority (*The Judgement of Martin Bucer*) to scriptural exegesis (*Tetrachordon*) and finally to invective (*Colasterion*). As Arthur Barker, among others, has pointed out, the divorce tracts mark Milton's break with the Presbyterian faction; for the first time in his career as a pamphlet writer he was proposing a course of action not sanctioned by the group whose causes he had supported. To maintain an unpopular position Milton drew upon all the resources of rhetoric and argument to which his reading and training gave him access. But the history of the divorce tracts is the history, in little, of Milton's disillusionment with men's willingness to listen to the voice of unassisted reason—hence their decline in appeals to reason as such. The failure of the divorce tracts to provoke any rational debate prefigures Milton's later more complete disappointment with human attraction to error.

But there is no doubt that the practical failure of the tracts in no way diminishes their importance for *Paradise Lost*. There were, of course, crucial differences of opinion between Milton and his contemporaries which would naturally hinder the success of the tracts as polemics. But the very ideas which could not gain wide acceptance in the controversy must have enriched for his audience Milton's treatment of marriage in *Paradise*

Lost. Both the prose works and the poem share the fundamental conviction that marriage requires a spiritual affinity of which the formal ceremony is merely the outward sign and on which the bodily conjunction of man and wife is dependent for its virtue, efficacy, and humanity. Milton's definition of marriage, his conception of woman, his notion of the matrimonial state, and his treatment of ideal marriage are coherent and mutually enlightening because of their insistence on this central dogma. Although his audience could deny the dogma legal application, it could not deny its aptness as an ideal. It is so treated in *Paradise Lost.* Furthermore, Milton necessarily gives sexual commerce in marriage a secondary role both in the tracts and in *Paradise Lost.* In the tracts, he is forced by his argument almost to underplay its urgency, but even in *Paradise Lost,* where he can safely praise matrimonial sexuality, he cannot give it absolute precedence, since sexuality before spiritual affinity and love would utterly subvert his and his audience's conception of the ideal marriage of Adam and Eve.

Milton's position in the tracts depends on an essential distinction between the rights of man and woman, based on the differences in their natural hierarchical level. This distinction is maintained also in *Paradise Lost,* in the critical and tragic disparity between the intellects of Adam and Eve, and in capacities for household prudence, mutual aid, authority, obedience, and love. Adam and Eve are differentiated for us, not only as ideal human types but as ideal man and woman, a distinction Milton never forgets. Each has peculiar strengths and potentialities, special virtues and characteristic sins. But the distinction has other implications as well. Passivity in the woman is not enough; in the tracts, failure to provide the response which is the wife's duty, prerogative, and proper pleasure—the reanimation and refreshment of the husband through interest, understanding, affection—is cause for divorce. In *Paradise Lost,* Eve's act of repentance precipitates the conversion of Adam from futile despair. In both the distinction of male and female and the use of marriage as an aid to salvation Milton reflects strong commonplace attitudes. The intimate relationship between personal emotion and human salvation is worked out in opposite ways in the tracts and in *Paradise Lost*—in the former negatively, in the latter positively. In *Paradise Lost* Milton can show not only how disruption and chaos follow and are reflected in matrimonial disharmony, but also how marriage can triumph over these very effects.

In the tracts, however, Milton also uses the differences between male and female to assert the primary individual right of the masculine partner to demand divorce if his marriage is unhappy. The individual nature establishes the standard of divine matrimonial law, blasphemously perverted by human law. Yet this emphasis upon human happiness in marriage as an essential feature of the divine plan, strange as it must have appeared in theoretical controversy, is one of the most brilliant and incontrovertible affirmations of *Paradise Lost,* where the marriage of Adam and Eve is the epitome of human delight. There the image of Adam and Eve, hand in hand, is a simultaneous emblem of happiness, mutuality, and order.

Paradise Lost is full of lessons about the place and effect of "ideas" in poetry. First of all, the poem enriches and renders meaningful concepts which may have only a limited and arguable value in exposition. Second, not only can Milton use conventional emblems such as the vine and the rib in a pronounced dramatic way, but he can also create new symbols to evoke particular associations: the bower of Adam and Eve becomes connected with the humanity of their love; the Garden becomes a consistent and subtle mirror image of their married happiness. Third, certain concepts emerge with greater clarity; one can guess more exactly from the behavior of Adam and Eve the proportion of physical and intellectual correspondence implied in the tracts by such a phrase as "amiable and attractive conversation." Finally, controversial positions are necessarily submerged by epic decorum, the decorum which demands authorial anonymity, a certain consonance between the opinions of poet and audience.

Milton in *Paradise Lost* has a chance to deal fully with moral issues more narrowly focused in the divorce tracts. The treatment of marriage in the poem is subtler, more suggestive, and more sound, for the full context of a concrete human situation is brought to bear upon that treatment. On one level, at least, *Paradise Lost* is a summary of human history, and in its double focus on the pain and the hopefulness of man's condition it passes a double judgment on woman and marriage. But as a Christian poem it also transcends tragedy through moral victory, and its final view even of the failure wrought by marriage is serene and triumphant.

Bibliography

The bibliography of primary sources includes the number of the work in the short-title catalogs and in Stillwell's catalog of incunabula. In the case of those few items for which I could find no entry I have indicated the location of the edition I have cited. A list of the abbreviations follows.

STC   A. W. Pollard and G. R. Redgrave, *A Short-Title Catalogue of Books Printed in England, Scotland, and Ireland and of English Books Printed Abroad, 1475–1640* (London, 1926)

Wing   Donald Wing, *Short-Title Catalogue of Books Printed in England, Scotland, Ireland, Wales, and British America and of English Books Printed in Other Countries, 1641–1700* (New York, 1945).

Stillwell Margaret Bingham Stillwell, *Incunabula in American Libraries, A Second Census* (New York, 1940).

L   British Museum, London.

Y   Beinecke Library, Yale University.

CN   Newberry Library, Chicago.

Primary Sources

Abbott, Robert, *A Christian Family Bvilded by God, Directing all Governours of Families how to act,* London, 1653. Wing A 68.

Agrippa, Henricus Cornelius, *The Glory of Women: or a Looking-Glasse for Ladies,* trans. H.C., London, 1652. Wing A 787.

[Allestree, Richard], *The Whole Duty of Man Necessary for all Families With Private Devotion for Seuerall Occasions,* London, 1660. L.

Ames, William, *Guiljelmi Amesij De Conscientia et eius iure, vel casi-
bus, libri quinque,* Amstelodami, 1631. L.
———, *The Marrow of Sacred Divinity,* London [1642]. Wing A 3000.
———, *Workes,* London, 1643. Wing A 2993.
Andrea, Johannes, *Summa Johannis Andreae de Sponsalibus et Matri-
moniis,* Rome [1490]. Stillwell A 571.
Antoninus Florentinus, *De Sponsalibus et Matrimonio,* Venice, 1474.
Stillwell A 684.
Argyle, Archibald Campbell, Marquis of, *Instructions to a Son,* Lon-
don, 1689. Wing A 3658.
Ariosto, Lodovico, *Ariostos Seven Planets Governing Itulie, or His
Satyrs,* London, 1611. STC 745.
Astell, Mary, *Some Reflections upon Marriage,* London, 1700. Wing A
4067.
B., A., *A Letter of Advice Concerning Marriage,* London, 1676. Wing
B 15.
Bacon, Francis, *Essayes or Counsels Civill and Morall,* ed. I. Gollancz,
London, 1901.
Barbaro, Francesco, *Directions for Love and Marriage,* London, 1677.
Y.
Baxter, Richard, *The Christian Directory, or A Summ of Practical
Theologie, and Cases of Conscience,* London, 1673. Wing B 1219.
Benlowes, Richard, *A Glance at the Glories of Sacred Friendship* [Lon-
don], 1657. Wing B 1872.
Bernard, Richard, *Ruths Recompence: or A Commentarie vpon the
Booke of Rvth . . . deliuered in seuerall sermons, the briefe summe
whereof is now published,* London, 1628. STC 1962.
Bible, Geneva, *The New Testament,* trans. into Latin from the Greek
and ed. Theodore Beza; trans. into English L. Thomson, London,
1583. STC 2885.
[Blake, William], *A Serious Letter Sent by a Private Christian to the
Lady Consideration,* London, 1655. Wing B 3153a.
B[lake], W[illiam], *The Triall of the Ladies, Hide Park, May Day,*
London, 1656. Wing B 3153b.
Boehme, Jakob, *Of the Election of Grace* in *The Works of Jacob
Behmen, Teutonic Theosopher,* trans. William Law, 4 vols. Lon-
don, 1764–81.
Bradshaw, William, *English Puritanisme,* London, 1641. Wing B 4158.
———, *A Mariage Feast,* London, 1620. STC 11680.
Brathwait, Richard, *The English Gentleman; and the English gentle-*

vvoman; both in one volvme couched, 3d ed. London, 1641. Wing
B 4262.

*A Brief Anatomie of Women: Being an Invective Against, and Apolo-
gie for, The Bad and Good of That Sexe*, London, 1653. Wing B
4524.

Brinsley, John, *A Looking-Glasse for Good Women*, London, 1645.
Wing B 4717.

Broxolme, Charles, *The good Old way: or, Perkins Improved, in a
Plain Exposition and Sound Application of Those Depths of Divinity briefly comprized in his Six Principles*, London, 1653. Wing B
5217.

Bullinger, Heinrich, *The Christian State of Matrimony*, trans. Myles
Coverdale, 6th ed. London, 1575. STC 4053.

Bunny, Edmund, *Of Divorce for adulterie*, Oxford, 1610. STC 4091.

Burghley, William Cecil, *Certain Precepts or directions for the well
ordering and cariage of a man's life*, London, 1617. (Another title:
Advice to His Son.) STC 4897.

Byfield, Nicholas, *A Commentary: or, Sermons vpon the Second Chapter of the First Epistle of Saint Peter*, London, 1623. STC 4211.

―――, *The Marrow of the Oracles of God*, 11th ed. London, 1640.
STC 4225.

Calvin, John, *Institutes of the Christian Religion*, trans. Floyd Lewis
Battles, 2 vols. Philadelphia [1961].

The Card of Courtship: or, the Language of Love, London, 1653. Wing
C 489.

Castiglione, Baldassare, *The Courtyer*, trans. Thomas Hoby, London,
1561. STC 4778.

*The City-Dames Petition In behalfe of the long afflicted, but well-
affected Cavaliers*, London, 1647. Wing C 4350.

Crompton, William, *A Wedding-Ring, Fitted to the Finger of Every
Paire That Have, or Shall Meete in the Feare of God: Or, That
divine circle of heavenly love, wherein man and wife should walke
all their dayes*, London, 1632. STC 6061.

Crooke, Samuel, *The Guide unto true blessednesse, or, A body of the
doctrine of the Scriptures directing man to the saving knowledge of
God*, 6th ed. London, 1640. STC 6068.

Dare, Josiah, *Counsellor Manners, His Last Legacy to His Son*, London, 1673. Wing D 247.

Dod, John, and Robert Cleaver, *A Godlie Forme of Household Government*, London, 1612. STC 5386.

————, *A Plaine and Familiar Exposition of the Ten Commandements,* London, 1609. STC 6971.

Donne, John, *Sermons,* ed. George Potter and E. M. Simpson, 10 vols. Berkeley, 1952–58.

An Elegie, and Epitaph for Mistris Abigail Sherard, London, 1648. Wing E 342.

Erasmus, Desiderius, *Christiani Matrimonii Institutio,* Inclyta Basilea, 1526. Y.

Eves, George, *The Churches Patience and Faith in Afflictions. Delivered in a Sermon at the Funerall of the Right Worshipfull, and Vertuous Cecilia Lady Peyton,* London, 1661. Wing E 3554.

Fisher, Joseph, *The Honour of Marriage: or, the Institution, Necessity, Advantage, Comforts, and Usefulness of a Married Life,* London, 1695. Wing F 1010.

Fuller, Thomas, *The Holy State and the Profane State,* ed. Maximilian Graff Walten, 2 vols. New York, 1938.

Gataker, Thomas, *A Good Wife Gods Gift,* London, 1637. STC 11661.

————, *Marriage Duties Briefly Couched Together,* London, 1637. STC 11668.

————, *A Marriage Prayer,* London, 1624. STC 11664.

[Gauden, John], *A Discourse of Auxiliary Beauty. Or Artificiall Hansomeness,* London, 1656. Wing G 355.

The Glasse of Godly Love, London, 1569. CN.

Gouge, William, *Of Domesticall Duties,* 2d ed. London, 1626. STC 12120.

Grantham, Thomas, *A Marriage Sermon,* London, 1643. Wing G 1555.

Grotius, Hugo, *Annotationes in Novum Testamentum,* Editio nova, 2 vols. Erlangae in Ptochotrophio et Lipsiae, 1755–57.

————, *Discourses: Of God, and His Providence; Of Christ, His Miracles and Doctrine,* trans. and ed. C. Barksdale, 2d ed. London, 1652. Wing G 2109.

Guild, William, *Loves Entercovrs between The Lamb & his Bride, Christ and his Church. Or, A clear Explication and Application of the Song of Solomon,* London, 1658. Wing G 2206.

H., I., *A Strange VVonder or VVonder in a VVoman,* London, 1642. Wing H 50.

H., T., *A Looking-Glasse for VVomen, or, A Spie for Pride,* London, 1644. Wing H 139.

Hammond, Henry, *A Paraphrase and Annotations Upon all the Books of the New Testament,* 2d ed. London, 1659. Wing H 573a.

————, *A Practical Catechisme*, London, 1646. Wing H 583.

Hardy, Nathanael, *Love and Fear The inseperable Twins Of A Blest Matrimony*, London, 1653. Wing H 732.

Herbert, William, *Herberts Careful Father and Pious Child*, London, 1648. Wing H 1539.

————, *Herberts Child-bearing Woman From the Conception to the Weaning of the Child*, London, 1648. Wing H 1540.

Hey Hoe, for a Husband, or, The Parliament of Maides, London, 1647. Wing H 1659.

Heydon, John, *Advice to a Daughter, In opposition to the Advice to a Son*, 2d ed. London, 1659. Wing H 1665.

Hieron, Samuel, *A Helpe vnto Deuotion*, London, 1610. Y.

————, *Sermons*, London, 1614–20. STC 13378.

Higford, William, *Institutions or Advice to His Grandson*, London, 1658. Wing H 1947.

H[ilder], T[homas], *Conjugall Counsell; or, Seasonable Advise, Both to Unmarried and Married Persons*, London, 1653. Wing H 1974.

Hill, William, *A New-Years-Gift for Women*, London, 1660. Wing H 2035.

Hooker, Richard, *Works*, ed. John Keble, 3d ed. 3 vols. Oxford, 1845.

The Honourable State of Matrimony made Comfortable, or an Antidote Against Discord Betwixt Man and Wife, London, 1685. Wing H 2601.

The Humble Petition of Many Thousands of Wives and Matrons of the City of London, and other parts of this Kingdome . . ., London, 1643. Wing H 3475.

An Invective Against the Pride of Women, [London], 1657. Wing I 284.

Jackson, Arthur, *Annotations Upon The five Books, immediately following the Historicall Part of the Old Testament*, London, 1658. Wing J 64.

King, John, *Vitis Palatina*, London, 1614. STC 14990.

L., W., *The Incomparable Jewell*, London, 1632. STC 15115.

L[onge], J., *An Epitaph on the late deceased, that truely-Noble and Renowned Lady Elizabeth Cromwel*, London, 1655. Wing L 2994.

The Maids Petition To the Honourable Members of both Houses . . . for their lawfull dayes of Recreation, London, 1647. Wing M 280.

Milton, John, *Complete Prose Works*, ed. Don M. Wolfe, 8 vols. New Haven, 1953–.

————, *Paradise Lost*, ed. Merritt Y. Hughes, New York, 1962.

More, Henry, *The Philosophick Cabbala* in *A Collection of Several Philosophical Writings of Dr. Henry More*, London, 1712–13.

Moore, Thomas, the Elder, *A Discovery of Seducers that creep into Houses*, London, 1646. Wing M 2593.

Needler, Benjamin, *Expository Notes, with Practical Observations, towards The opening of the five first Chapters of the first Book of Moses called Genesis*, London, 1655. Wing N 412.

[Nevile, Henry,] *The Ladies Parliament* [London, 1647]. Wing N 508.

——, *The Ladies, A Second Time, Assembled in Parliament* [London], 1647. Wing N 507.

Nevizzano, Giovanni, *Silua Nuptialis bonis referta non modicis*, Paris, 1521. L.

Niccholes, Alexander, *A Discourse of Marriage and Wiving* (London, 1615) in *Harleian Miscellany*, 2 (1809), 156–82.

Now or Never: Or, A New Parliament of Women, London, 1656. Wing N 1656.

Osborn, Francis, *Advice to a Son*, 8th ed. London, 1682. Wing O 506.

Packington, Lady Dorothy, *The Whole Duty of Man Necessary for all Families With Private Devotion for Seuerall Occasions*, London, 1660. (Same as Allestree, Richard, above.) L.

Paget, Thomas (Theophilus Philoparnus), *A Religiovs Scrvtiny Concerning Vnequal Marriage*, London, 1649. Wing P 169.

The Parliament of VVomen, London, 1646. Wing P 505.

Parsons, Bartholemew, *Boaz and Rvth Blessed Or A Sacred Contract Honovred with a solemne Benediction*, Oxford, 1633. STC 19345.

Penn, William, *The Fruits of a Father's Love*, London, 1730.

Perkins, William, *Christian Oeconomie: or, a Short Survey of the Right Manner of Ordering a Familie according to the Scriptures*, London, 1609. STC 19677.

——, *Works*, Cambridge, 1603. STC 19647.

——, *Works*, 3 vols. London, 1626–31. STC 19652, 19653, 19653a.

Pettie, George, *A Petite Pallace of Pettie His Pleasure*, Oxford, 1938 (London, 1576).

Polyandrus, Johannes, A. Rivetus, A. Walaeus, and A. Thysius, *Synopsis Purioris Theologiae*, Lugdunus Batavorum, 1632. CN.

Poole, Matthew, *Annotations upon the Holy Bible*, 2 vols. London, 1683–85. Wing P 2820.

Poulain de la Barre, François, *The Woman as Good as the Man: or the Equallity of Both Sexes*, trans. A. L., London, 1677. Wing P 3038.

The Practical Part of Love, London, 1660. Wing P 3154.

Preston, John, *The Breast-Plate of Faith and Love,* 3d ed. London, 1632. STC 20211.

————, *The Churches Marriage; or Dignitie,* London, 1638. STC 20227.

Ralegh, Sir Walter, *Advice to his Son: his Sons advice to his Father,* London, 1675. Wing R 184.

A Remonstrance of the Shee-Citizens of London, London, 1647. Wing R 1014.

Reyner, Edmund, *Precepts for Christian Practice: Or the Rule of the New Creature,* London, 1645. Wing R 1223.

Reynolds, Edward, *Mary Magdalens Love to Christ. Opened in a Sermon Preached at the Funeral of Mistris Elizabeth Thomason,* London, 1659. Wing R 1264.

Rivetus, Andreas, *Praelectiones in Cap. xx Exodi,* Editio Secunda, Lugduni Batavorvm, 1637. L.

Robinson, John, *An Appendix to Mr. Perkins his Six Principles of Christian Religion,* London, 1656. Wing R 1692.

————, *Works,* ed. Robert Ashton, 3 vols. Boston, 1851.

Robotham, John, *An Exposition On the whole booke of Solomons Song, Commonly called the Canticles,* London, 1651. Wing R 1730.

Rogers, Daniel, *Matrimoniall Honovr: or, The mutuall Crowne and comfort of godly, loyall, and chaste Marriage,* London, 1642, Wing R 1797.

Rogers, Richard, *A Commentary vpon the Whole Booke of Judges,* London, 1615. STC 21204.

Rous, Francis, *The Misticall Marriage Betweene Christ and His Church,* London, 1653. Wing R 2024.

S[andys], G[eorge], *A Paraphrase vpon the Song of Solomon,* London, 1642. Wing B 2629b.

Secker, William, *A Wedding Ring Fit for the Finger: Or, the salve of Divinity On the sore of Humanity,* London, 1658. Wing S 2254.

Selden, John, *De Jure Naturali et Gentium,* London, 1640. STC 22168.

Shaw, John, *Mistris Shawes Tomb-stone, Or, The Saints Remains,* London, 1658. Wing S 3029.

Sibbes, Richard, *Beames of Divine Light* . . . , London, 1639. STC 22475.

————, *The Gloriovs Feast of the Gospel,* London, 1650. Wing S 3736.

————, *Works,* ed. John C. Miller, 7 vols. Edinburgh, 1862–64.

Smith, Henry, *Sermons,* London, 1622. STC 22731.

Spencer, Benjamin,'Αφωνόλογος.A Dumb Speech; Or, a Sermon made but no Sermon preached, at the Funerall of the Right Vertuous, Mrs Mary Overman, London, 1646. Wing S 4942.

Spinckes, Samuel, A Hand-Kercheffe for a Disconsolate Soule, to wipe away his Sinne, and to keep him from Despaire, as though they had never been committed, London, 1651. Wing S 4980.

A Spiritual Journey Of A Young Man, towards the Land of Peace, to live therein Essentially in God, London, 1659. Wing S 4998.

Stalham, John, Vindiciae Redemptionis in the Fanning and Sifting of Samvel Oates, London, 1647. Wing S 5187.

Stock, Richard, A Commentary upon the Prophecy of Malachi, ed. Alexander B. Grosart, Edinburgh, 1865.

Taylor, Jeremy, The Whole Works, ed. Reginald Heber, 15 vols. London, 1822.

Taylor, Thomas, A Good Hvsband and A Good Wife, London, 1625. STC 23829.

———, Works, ed. Edm. Calamy, A. Jackson, S. Ash, et al., London, 1653. Wing T 560.

Temple, Sir Peter, Mans Master-piece: Or, the Best Improvement of the worst Condition, London, 1658. Wing T 632.

Thorowgood, G., Pray be not Angry: Or, the Womens New Law, London, 1656. Wing T 1064.

Tilney, Edmund, A brief and pleasant discourse of duties in Mariage, called the Flower of Friendshippe, London, 1568. STC 24076.

T[yping], W[illiam], The Fathers Covnsell: Or, Certain Usefull Directions, for all young persons, especially elder Brothers, whose portion it is or may be, in these perilous daies, to be left in a Fatherlesse or Friendlesse Condition, London, 1644. Wing T 3565.

Ussher, James, A Body of Divinity, London, 1648. Wing U 153.

Vauts, Moses à, The Husband's Authority Unvail'd; wherein It is moderately discussed whether it be fit or lawfull for a good Man, to beat his bad Wife, London, 1650. Wing V 163.

Vertue, Henry, Christ and the Church: or Parallels in Three Books, London, 1659. Wing V 274.

The Virgins Complaint for the losse of their Sweet-Hearts, by these present Wars, And their owne long solitude and keeping their Virginities against their Wills, London, 1642. Wing V 640.

Vives, Joannes Ludovicus Valentinus (Juan Luis Vives), De Officio Mariti. Liber Unus. De Institutione Foeminae Christianae Libri

tres. *De Ingenvorum Adolescentum Puellarum Institutione Libri duo*, Basileae, 1540. CN.
———, *The Instruction of a Christen Woman*, trans. Richard Hyrde, London, 1557. STC 24861.
———, *The Office and Duetie of an Husband*, trans. Thomas Paynell, London [1555?]. STC 24855.
Warren, John, *Principles of Christian Doctrine*, London, 1654. Wing W 977.
Whately, William, *A Bride-Bush: Or, A Wedding Sermon: Compendiously describing the duties of Married Persons*, London, 1617. STC 25296.
———, *A Care-cloth: Or A Treatise of the Cvmbers and Trovbles of Marriage*, . . . London, 1624. STC 25299.
Whatman, Edward, *Funerall Obseqvies, to the Right Honourable the Lady Elizabeth Hopton*, London, 1647. Wing W 1591.
The Widovves Lamentation for the Absence of their deare Children, and Suitors, London, 1643. Wing W 2093.
Wilkinson, Robert, *The Merchant Royall*, London, 1615. STC 25660.
Wing, John, *The Crowne Conjugall or, The Spouse Royall*, Middleburgh, 1620. STC 25844.

Secondary Sources

Axelrad, Arthur M., "One Gentle Stroking: Milton on Divorce," doctoral dissertation, New York University, 1962.
Barker, Arthur, *Milton and the Puritan Dilemma, 1641–1660*, Toronto, 1942.
Camden, Charles Carroll, *The Elizabethan Woman*, London, 1952.
Demetz, Peter, "The Elm and the Vine: Notes Toward a Definition of a Marriage Topos," *PMLA*, 73 (1958), 521–32.
Didbin, Sir Lewis, and Sir Charles E. H. C. Healey, *English Church Law and Divorce*, London, 1912.
Fletcher, Harris F., *The Use of the Bible in Milton's Prose*, University of Illinois Studies in Language and Literature, 14, 3, Urbana, 1929.
French, Joseph Milton, *The Life Records of John Milton*, New Brunswick, N.J., 1950.
Frye, Roland M., "The Teachings of Classical Puritanism on Conjugal Love," in *Studies in the Renaissance* (Renaissance Society of America), 2 (1955), 148–59.

George, Charles H. and Katherine, *The Protestant Mind of the English Reformation, 1570–1640,* Princeton, 1961.

Gilman, Wilbur Elwyn, *Milton's Rhetoric: Studies in His Defense of Liberty,* University of Missouri Studies, 14, 3, Columbia, Mo., 1939.

Haller, William, *The Rise of Puritanism,* New York, 1938.

———, "Hail Wedded Love," *English Literary History, 13* (1946), 79–97.

———, *Liberty and Reformation in the Puritan Revolution,* New York, 1955.

Haller, William and Malleville, "The Puritan Art of Love," *Huntington Library Quarterly, 5* (1942), 235–72.

Hanford, James Holly, *John Milton, Englishman,* New York, 1949.

Kelley, Maurice W., *This Great Argument: A Study of Milton's* De Doctrina Christiana *as a Gloss upon* Paradise Lost, Princeton Studies in English, 22, Princeton, 1941.

Kelso, Ruth, *Doctrine for the Lady of the Renaissance,* Urbana, Ill., 1956.

———, *The Doctrine of the English Gentleman in the Sixteenth Century,* University of Illinois Studies, 14, 1929.

Knappen, Marshall Mason, *Tudor Puritanism: A Chapter in the History of Idealism,* Chicago, 1939.

Kranidas, Thomas, *The Fierce Equation: A Study of Milton's Decorum,* The Hague, 1965.

Larson, Martin Alfred, *The Modernity of Milton,* Chicago, 1927.

Lewis, Clive Staples, *A Preface to* Paradise Lost, London, 1942.

Mason, John Edward, *Gentlefolk in the Making,* Philadelphia, 1935.

Mitchell, William Fraser, *English Pulpit Oratory from Andrewes to Tillotson,* London, 1932.

Moody, Lester Deane, ed., "John Milton's Pamphlets on Divorce," doctoral dissertation, University of Washington, 1956.

Morgan, Edmund S., *The Puritan Family: Essays on Religion and Domestic Relations in Seventeenth-Century New England,* Boston, 1944.

———, *Visible Saints: The History of a Puritan Idea,* New York, 1963.

Nicolson, Marjorie, *John Milton: A Reader's Guide to His Poetry,* New York, 1963.

Powell, Chilton Latham, *English Domestic Relations, 1487–1653,* New York, 1917.

Rajan, Balachandre, *"Paradise Lost" and the Seventeenth-Century Reader,* London, 1947.

Svendsen, Kester, "Science and Structure in Milton's *Doctrine of Divorce*," *PMLA*, *67* (1952), 435–45.

Williams, Arnold, *The Common Expositor: An Account of the Commentaries on Genesis, 1527–1633*, Chapel Hill, 1948.

Wright, Louis B., *Middle Class Culture in Elizabethan England*, Chapel Hill, 1935.

Index

82; preaching of, 76; beauty of, 76, 81, 106, 117–19; superiority of, 76–79, 81, 106, 110; responsibility for Fall, 77–78, 82, 113–31; education of, 79–81; strength of, 79, 87; defense of, 81–82; ambivalence toward, 82; fragility of, 85; symbols of: *see* Glass, Venetian; Rib; Serpent; Vine. *See also* Eve

Wright, Louis B., vii

Zenobia, 65 n.